Esther

Esther and her relative Mordecai are depicted in this 17th century painting by the Dutch artist Aert van Gelder. The book of Esther describes the origins of a joyous Jewish celebration known as Purim.

Money at its Best: Millionaires of the Bible

Abraham and Sarah	Joseph
Daniel	Moses
David	Noah
Esther	Samson
Jacob	Solomon
Job	Wealth in Biblical Times

Esther

Stephen B. Woodruff

Mason Crest Publishers
Philadelphia

Produced by OTTN Publishing.
Cover design © 2009 TLC Graphics, www.TLCGraphics.com.

Mason Crest Publishers
370 Reed Road, Suite 302
Broomall PA 19008
www.masoncrest.com

Copyright © 2009 by Mason Crest Publishers. All rights reserved.
Printed and bound in the United States of America.

First printing

1 3 5 7 9 8 6 4 2

Library of Congress Cataloging-in-Publication Data

  Woodruff, Stephen B.
   Esther / Stephen B. Woodruff.
     p. cm. — (Millionaires of the Bible)
   Includes bibliographical references.
   ISBN 978-1-4222-0469-6 (hc)
   ISBN 978-1-4222-0844-1 (pbk.)
  1. Esther, Queen of Persia—Juvenile literature. 2. Bible. O.T.—Biography—Juvenile literature. I. Title.
  BS580.E8W66 2008
  222'.9092—dc22
                                            2008020864

Publisher's Note: The Web sites listed in this book were active at the time of publication. The publisher is not responsible for Web sites that have changed their address or discontinued operation since the date of publication. The publisher reviews and updates the Web sites each time the book is reprinted.

Table of Contents

Esther and Her Wealth   6
Introduction: Wealth and Faith   7
1. The Scroll   11
2. In Search of a Queen   27
3. Haman's Revenge   45
4. A Time to Mourn   57
5. Dinner for Three   66
6. An Unexpected Development   73
7. Justice and an Unstoppable Edict   82
8. From Battle Day to Holiday   91

Notes   104
Glossary   109
Further Reading   111
Internet Resources   113
Index   115
Illustration Credits   119
About the Author   120

Esther and Her Wealth

- Esther, a beautiful Jewish maiden, was chosen from hundreds of young women to be the Persian king's new queen. As the king's wife, she now had access to the best of everything. Esther's true wealth, however, was in her faith and her determination to help her people.

- When Esther heard from her relative Mordecai about Haman's plot to kill the Jews, she was devastated. She quickly issued orders to Mordecai: "Go, gather together all the Jews who are in Susa, and fast for me. Do not eat or drink for three days, night or day. I and my maids will fast as you do. When this is done, I will go to the king, even though it is against the law. And if I perish, I perish" (Esther 4:16). Even though she was queen, she risked certain death if the king did not recognize her while he was sitting on his throne. All the gold in the kingdom would not save her if the king rejected her.

- Ancient Hebrew texts describe how Esther dressed in the most expensive clothes and jewels she owned as she prepared to go before the king. She wore diamonds and other precious stones, as well as luxurious linens—clothes that were truly fit for a queen!

- With Mordecai's help, Queen Esther successfully thwarted the plot to kill the Jews, and Haman was put to death. According to the Bible and Jewish legends, the king gave Esther Haman's estate, making her even wealthier.

- Esther was the richest woman in Persia. However, she did not keep her material possessions to herself. "And Mordecai came into the presence of the king, for Esther had told how he was related to her. The king took off his signet ring, which he had reclaimed from Haman, and presented it to Mordecai. And Esther appointed him over Haman's estate." (Esther 8:1-2)

- Esther's ability to face adversity, even if it meant certain death for herself, was her greatest treasure.

Introduction: Wealth and Faith

Many people believe strongly that great personal wealth is incompatible with deep religious belief—that like oil and water, the two cannot be mixed. Christians, in particular, often feel this way, recollecting Jesus Christ's own teachings on wealth. "Do not store up for yourselves treasures on earth, where moth and rust destroy, and where thieves break in and steal," Jesus cautions during the Sermon on the Mount (Matthew 6:19). In Luke 18:25, he declares, "It is easier for a camel to go through the eye of a needle than for a rich man to enter the kingdom of God"—a sentiment repeated elsewhere in the Gospels.

Yet in Judeo-Christian culture there is a long-standing tradition of material wealth as the manifestation of God's blessing. This tradition is amply reflected in the books of the Hebrew Bible (or as Christians know them, the Old Testament). Genesis 13:2 says that the patriarch Abram (Abraham) "had become very wealthy in livestock and in silver and gold"; the Bible makes it clear that this prosperity is a gift from God. Other figures whose lives are chronicled in

Genesis—including Isaac, Jacob, Joseph, Noah, and Job—are described as both wealthy and righteous. The book of Deuteronomy expresses God's promise of prosperity for those who obey his commandments:

> If you fully obey the Lord your God and carefully follow all his commands I give you today, the Lord your God will set you high above all the nations on earth. . . . The Lord will grant you abundant prosperity—in the fruit of your womb, the young of your livestock and the crops of your ground—in the land he swore to your forefathers to give you. (Deuteronomy 28:1, 11)

A key requirement for this prosperity, however, is that God's blessings must be used to help others. Deuteronomy 15:10–11 says, "Give generously . . . and do so without a grudging heart; then because of this the Lord your God will bless you in all your work and in everything you put your hand to." The book of Proverbs—written during the time of Solomon, one of history's wealthiest rulers—similarly presents wealth as a desirable blessing that can be obtained through hard work, wisdom, and following God's laws. Proverbs 14:31 promises, "The faithless will be fully repaid for their ways, and the good man rewarded for his."

Numerous stories and folktales show the generosity of the patriarchs. According to Jewish legend, Job owned an inn at a crossroads, where he allowed travelers to eat and drink at no cost. When they offered to pay, he instead told them about God, explaining that he was simply a steward of the wealth that God had given to him and urging them to worship God, obey God's commands, and receive their own blessings. A story about Abraham says that when he moved his flocks from one field to another, he would muzzle the animals so that they would not graze on a neighbor's property.

After the death of Solomon, however, the kingdom of Israel

was divided and the people fell away from the commandments God had mandated. The later writings of the prophets, who are attempting to correct misbehavior, specifically address unethical acts committed to gain wealth. "You trample on the poor," complained the prophet Amos. "You oppress the righteous and take bribes and you deprive the poor of justice in the courts" (Amos 5:11, 12). The prophet Isaiah insists, "Learn to do right! Seek justice, encourage the oppressed. . . . If you are willing and obedient, you will eat the best from the land; but if you resist and rebel, you will be devoured by the sword" (Isaiah 1:17, 19–20).

Viewed in this light, the teachings of Jesus take on new meaning. Jesus does not condemn wealth; he condemns those who would allow the pursuit of wealth to come ahead of the proper relationship with God: "No one can serve two masters. . . . You cannot serve both God and money" (Matthew 6:24).

Today, nearly everyone living in the Western world could be considered materially wealthier than the people of the Bible, who had no running water or electricity, lived in tents, walked when traveling long distances, and wore clothing handmade from animal skins. But we also live in an age when tabloid newspapers and trashy television programs avidly follow the misadventures of spoiled and selfish millionaire athletes and entertainers. In the mainstream news outlets, it is common to read or hear reports of corporate greed and malfeasance, or of corrupt politicians enriching themselves at the expense of their constituents. Often, the responsibility of the wealthy to those members of the community who are not as successful seems to have been forgotten.

The purpose of the series MONEY AT ITS BEST: MILLIONAIRES OF THE BIBLE is to examine the lives of key figures from biblical history, showing how these people used their wealth or their powerful and privileged positions in order to make a difference in the lives of others.

For Jews, the story of Esther is a tale of salvation. Across the ages, Jews have held Esther's courage, determination, and strength of personality in high regard.

The Scroll

The book of Esther tells the story of a beautiful young Jewish girl who rises to great power when she becomes the wife of the Persian king, Ahasuerus (Xerxes). The book, located in the Tanakh (Hebrew Bible) just after the Book of Ecclesiastes, and in the Christian Old Testament following the books of Ezra and Nehemiah, belongs to scripture classified as "The Writings" (in Hebrew, *ketuvim*).

To Jews, Esther is a great hero. Her scroll is the last of the Five Festal Scrolls, after Lamentations, Ruth, Song of Songs, and Ecclesiastes. Jews read the entire Scroll of Esther once a year during the rousing, raucous, much-loved festival of Purim (Lots). The events told in the book of Esther purport to be the history behind the first Purim celebration. Esther is so beloved the only appellation needed for her story is, in Hebrew, *hamm'gillah*: The Scroll. Ancient Jewish sages maintained that in the days after the coming of the Messiah, all of the holy writings would pass away except for the Law and the scroll of Esther.

Christians have less experience with the book of Esther. Purim is not a Christian festival, and Esther is one of the few Old Testament books never quoted in the New Testament scriptures. In the Revised Common Lectionary, a widely used ecumenical list of readings for weekly worship, a scripture lesson from the book of Esther appears once every three years; eleven verses are read—barely a sampling of the book, along with three other readings for the day. Biblical commentator Carol M. Bechtel writes, "We can no longer assume that the [non-Jewish] congregation already knows the story. . . . We cannot rely on the lectionary to acquaint [them] with the book of Esther. . . . Could it be that one of the reasons we do not give the book of Esther more 'airtime' is that we simply do not know what to say about it?"

THE STORY IN SUMMARY

The scriptures used by Jews (the Hebrew Bible, or Tanakh) is also known as the Masoretic text. The Masoretic text (MT)—named to delineate it from earlier versions of the scriptures—is attributed to the Masoretes, a group of scribes and scholars that worked in the seventh through tenth centuries C.E. (The Hebrew word *mesorah* refers to the transmission of tradition.) The story of Esther in the MT is this: Vashti, the reigning Queen of Persia, disobeys a command of Ahasuerus the

Ornate silver case used to store the megillah, or scroll, of Esther.

Ruins at Persepolis, the capital of the Persian Empire during the time period depicted in Esther. In 586 B.C.E., the kingdom of Judah had been conquered by the armies of the Mesopotamian ruler Nebuchadnezzar; he ordered the Jewish temple to be destroyed and the Jews led to captivity in Babylon. The Babylonian captivity lasted until about 539 B.C.E., when the Persians conquered Babylon. After this, the Persian ruler Cyrus the Great granted Jews permission to return to their homes in Judah. Tens of thousands did return, as described in the Biblical books Ezra and Nehemiah; however, many Jews remained in Persia or Babylon. These regions (modern-day Iraq and Iran) maintained significant Jewish communities until the state of Israel was established in the mid–20th century.

king and is subsequently deposed. The king's advisors recommend he summon all the young women of the Kingdom in order to find a suitable replacement—someone he finds attractive. All the young women in the kingdom are rounded up, including Esther, a Jew, whose cousin and guardian, Mordecai, has warned her to keep her Jewish heritage a secret. After a year of preparation, Ahasuerus chooses Esther to be his queen. Esther moves from the middle class to millionaire status. Soon afterward, Mordecai foils a plot to kill the king.

In his job at the palace gate, Mordecai runs afoul of Haman, the king's grand vizier, who decides not only to punish Mordecai the Jew for his behavior, but to annihilate all the Jews living in the Kingdom. Haman tricks the king into agreeing to the eradication. Haman's soothsayers cast a lot (*pur*) to determine the date of the slaughter. The pogrom is scheduled eleven months from that day.

Through a series of coincidences, reversals, and other ironic occurrences, Esther exposes Haman's plot and prevents the genocide; all is well in the Kingdom once more. Purim becomes the official celebration of the Jews' salvation from annihilation at Haman's hand.

Many Versions and Changes

The MT version of the Esther story is also the one known to Protestant Christians. Protestants adopted the Masoretic text as the basis for their Old Testament.

Roman Catholics and Eastern Orthodox Christians use another version of the text, the Septuagint, as the basis for their Old Testament scriptures. The Septuagint is a Greek translation of the Hebrew scriptures, made between the third and first centuries B.C.E. It is therefore older than the Masoretic text, although both draw on the same stories, transmitted orally for generations by Israelite priests and Jewish rabbis. Overall, the Septuagint and Masoretic translations are very similar; however, there are some differences. The Septuagint version of the book of Esther contains six Additions (a total of 107 verses), which alter the tone of the book. The ancient translator/editors of the Septuagint saw a great deficiency in the ancient Hebrew text of the Esther story. There is no direct mention of God, of God's name, or of God's activity and influence in the original Hebrew version. So, the Additions strive to make the book of Esther more religious in nature.

When the fourth century Church Father Jerome translated the Bible into Latin (the Vulgate), he was unable to find Hebrew manuscripts that could authenticate the six Additions. He pulled them out of the text and placed them at the end of his translation.

After the Protestant Reformation of the 16th century, as Church reformers created their own version of the Biblical canon, they moved the additions away from the book of Esther altogether, placing them in the Apocrypha under the title "Additions to the Book of Esther." The Roman Catholic response to this action was to affirm the position of the apocryphal (they termed them "deutero-canonical") books in their canon. Older translations of the Roman Catholic Bible place the Additions as Chapters 11–16 in Esther, after the story as it had appeared in the Masoretic text (Hebrew Bible), and out of context with

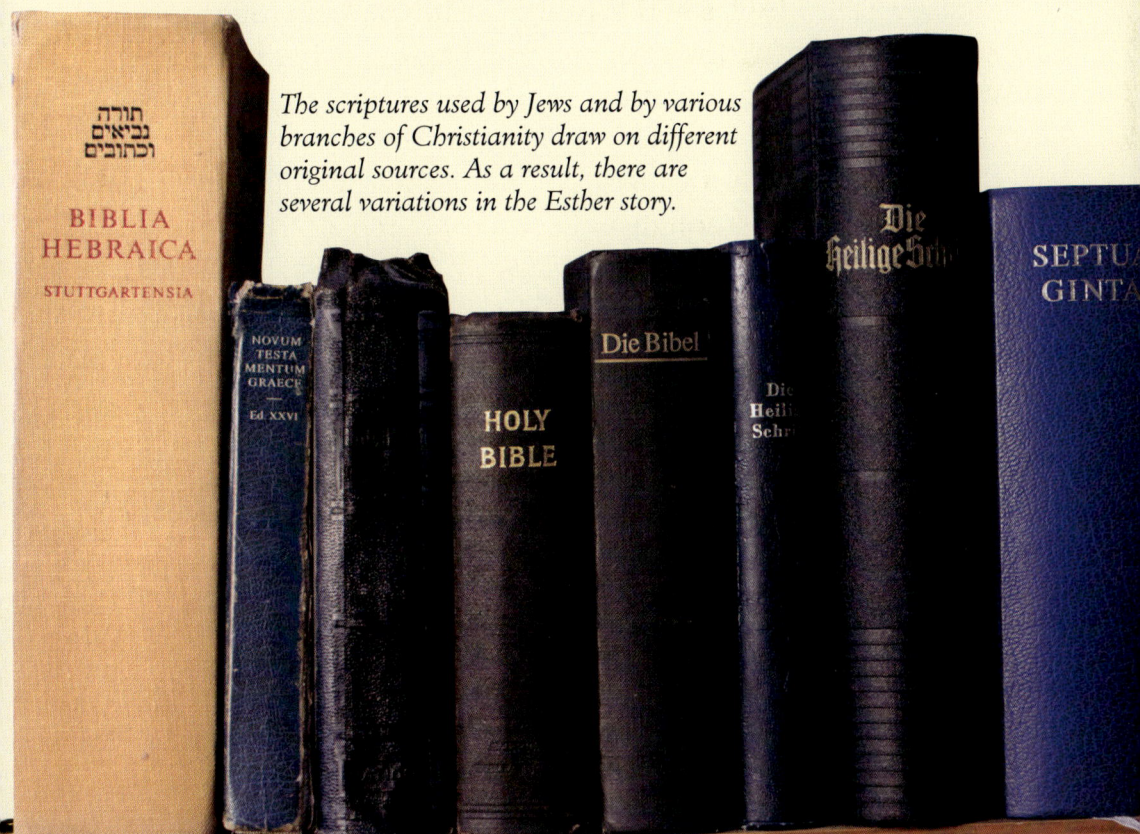

The scriptures used by Jews and by various branches of Christianity draw on different original sources. As a result, there are several variations in the Esther story.

16 *Esther*

the action. The New American Bible, one of the translations used by Catholics today, integrates the Additions into the story, as they had appeared in the Septuagint. The placement of the Additions in other modern Bibles varies with the translations.

After careful examination, scholars today are convinced that different authors are responsible for writing the Additions. These author/editors added them to the text at different times. By studying the use of certain words and phrases, scholars have determined that

The reformer Martin Luther reluctantly included Esther in his 1534 edition of the Bible. Luther once wrote, "I am so hostile to ... Esther that I could wish [it] did not exist at all; for [it] judaize[s] too greatly and [has] much pagan impropriety." By "judaize," Luther meant that the book indicates that Christians should follow the 613 laws set forth in the Torah, or first five books of the Old Testament.

at least two of the Additions originated in Greek, and were not translated from an older Hebrew account.

ANCIENT ROOTS OF ESTHER

Biblical scholars have studied the various versions of Esther in order to understand their origins. "Like most of the Bible, the book of Esther did not appear out of nowhere, born full-grown in its present form; nor did its growth stop with that form," writes Michael V. Fox, a professor of Hebrew studies at the University of Wisconsin. "In the case of Esther we have not only some of the ancient retellings—notably the Septuagint (LXX), Josephus' paraphrase, Targum Sheni [a version of the Esther story written in Aramaic], and the Old Latin (translated from a Greek version)—but also a version that . . . is earlier than or at least independent of the MT. This is the proto-AT, the earliest layer of the Greek Alpha text (AT)."

By a close analysis of the texts available in their original languages, Fox supposes that a seed story existed in Hebrew prior to any of the existing written accounts. He calls this source, which was used as the basis for the written versions, "Proto-Esther." According to Fox, Proto-Esther gave rise to two versions in Hebrew, which he identifies as proto-AT (for Alpha-text) and MT (the Masoretic text). One branch, the MT, remained in the version known today as the Hebrew Scripture, but was also translated into Greek, receiving six additions over time, referred to by scholars as Additions A through F; this became the Septuagint version. Moving down the second branch, another editor combined the proto-AT text with other material from the Septuagint, plus the Additions, and created the version Fox calls the Alpha Text. "The AT is preserved in five Greek [manuscripts] dating from the tenth to thirteenth centuries C.E.," Fox states. Thus, the work of many ancient authors and editors resulted in the versions of the book of Esther available in modern times.

DATE OF ORIGIN

Because the story in the book of Esther is set in the Persian Empire and talks about King Ahasuerus (traditionally identified as Xerxes I, ruler of Persia from 485 to 465 B.C.E.) as a main character, scholars generally agree that the story was written after that time, perhaps between 400 and 200 B.C.E. At one time, some Bible scholars believed the patriotic feeling expressed in the book meant that it had been written during the Maccabean Period (167–135 B.C.E.), a time of great nationalistic fervor among Jews as they rose up against Greco-Syrian oppression. However, that view is largely abandoned today.

Adele Berlin, a professor of Hebrew Bible at the University of Maryland, dates the book of Esther to a time when Greek writers wrote extensively about the Persian Empire and their work was widely available, during the fifth and fourth centuries B.C.E. She writes,

> Indeed, the author of Esther seems to have been very familiar with the kinds of stories and motifs that occur in the Greek writings about Persia during the Persian period, and that may have been conventional literary fare at that time. I am not suggesting that the author of Esther read the Greek stories, only that the Greek writers and our author drew on a similar collection of narrative motifs.

Berlin dates Esther's writing to between 400 and 335 B.C.E.—after the historical Xerxes but before the Greeks conquered Persia under Alexander the Great.

The authorship of the original story is unknown. The words in Esther 9:20, "Mordecai recorded these things," prompted traditional interpreters to identify Mordecai as the author. However, modern scholars agree that the real author can never be known. Much evidence suggests the story was written in Persia: the details of Persian court life, the Persian words and names, the knowledge of the political structure and of the interprovince messaging system seem to be historically accurate. Perhaps the story was written in or around Susa, the Persian city in which the story is set, by a Jew living there during the late days of the Persian Empire, but it is impossible to know.

ENTRY INTO THE CANON

A Canon of Scripture is a list of writings that members of a religious group consider to be authoritative and inspired by God. Jews and various Christian denominations each have their own versions of the Biblical Canon. The process of developing the Canon cannot be localized to a single meeting time and place; instead, it takes place over many decades or centuries.

According to some interpreters, the book of Esther's admission to the Jewish Canon of Scripture came late due to the controversial fact that God is not featured in the book. This was the subject of much debate among the Jewish rabbis who put the canon in its final form during the first, second, and third centuries C.E. Also missing from the story of Esther are characteristics of books that were always considered part of the Hebrew canon: examples of Jewish piety, dietary laws, the covenant, and regular prayer to an omnipresent God. Many rabbis doubted it was divinely inspired.

The Essene community at Qumran did not include the book of Esther in its canon; Esther is the only book of the

Hebrew Bible not found among the Dead Sea Scrolls. Some scholars feel this is an archaeological accident—the scroll may have been hidden, but simply was not found with the rest of the ancient texts. But Gettysburg College professor of religion Carey Moore, in his commentary on Esther, cites the work of two scholars, Ginsberg and Bardtke, who believe Esther was rejected by the Qumran community for theological reasons. "Perhaps the Essenes resented the absence of any explicit mention of God in the book; or possibly they did not consider Esther a 'good' Jewess because she failed to observe the laws of *kashrut*," writes Moore. (*Kashrut* refers to Jewish dietary laws.) Moore argues that Esther was probably added to the Hebrew Bible canon by the Council of Jamnia in 90 C.E.

If Jews questioned the canonical status of Esther, so too did Christians. In the Western centers of early Christianity (Hippo, Carthage, Rome, Jerusalem, and Damascus), Esther was usually considered part of the canon; in the Eastern centers (Sardis, Iconium, Nazianzus, and Alexandria) it was not. Church leaders in Constantinople held both views. Many Christian Church Fathers associated Esther with the books of Judith and Tobit, two apocryphal works. Without the Additions in the Septuagint to make the book more overtly religious, the story of Esther appears to be about a Jewish festival not observed by Christians. Parts of the Esther story were criticized as being too violent and needlessly bloodthirsty, and at times anti-Gentile. Modern-day Christians still struggle to find meaning in the book.

ETIOLOGY FOR PURIM

Most modern scholars acknowledge Esther is a work of fiction, written as an etiology, or explanation, for Purim. Purim may have been celebrated by Jews in the

The caves at Qumran, where the Dead Sea Scrolls were discovered during the 1940s and 1950s. The ancient scrolls, some dating to 150 B.C.E., were the library of a conservative Jewish sect called the Essenes. The Qumran community of Essenes lived apart from other Jews, attempting to experience "eternal life" in their earthly lives. They had strong apocalyptic beliefs about the eventual end of the world. The Dead Sea Scrolls include most books of the Hebrew Bible. Part of the scrolls' importance lies in the fact that as the earliest known texts they are practically identical to the modern texts of the Bible. This shows that the Bible was essentially in its finished form by the second century B.C.E. However, Esther was not found among the Dead Sea Scrolls, indicating that the sect may not have accepted the book as divinely inspired.

years following the exile in Babylon (586 B.C.E.) and during the later dispersion throughout the Persian Empire.

With its cast of memorable characters, the book of Esther sounds like history. The Persians conquered the Babylonians in 539 B.C.E., allowing those Jews who wished to do so to return home. Since Purim is not mentioned in the Jewish law (the Torah); and all other Jewish festivals have their basis in some historic event, justification for the celebration was necessary. Jews may have

Israeli Jews parade in costumes as part of a Purim celebration. Purim is celebrated each year in February or March; the date varies because it is fixed in the Hebrew calendar, which uses both the moon and the sun to establish months. Purim is celebrated by a public reading of Esther, followed by charitable giving, sharing of gifts, and a festive meal.

adopted a Purim-like festival while in exile, then shared it with their neighbors, passing it along so it spread among the Jews "back home." Purim's joyous nature, its wild freedom to feast and drink and make merry endeared it to the celebrants; they couldn't let it go. They needed a story to explain it. Adele Berlin writes, "This story seems to have been known in several different versions, or to have gone through a number of different stages in its development before it was linked with Purim and incorporated in the Bible."

PARALLELS WITH OTHER LITERATURE

Careful literary analysis gives reason to doubt the historical nature of Esther. Evidence suggests that the author of the story patterned it closely in language, theme, and setting to the Joseph stories in Genesis. The wording, as analyzed by scholar Sandra Beth Berg, is strikingly similar in the Hebrew, utilizing the same words in similar contexts. One such example is the elevation of Joseph to greatness compared to the elevation of Mordecai to greatness. Genesis 41:42–43, Berg's translation, reads, "and he arrayed . . . and had him ride . . . and they cried out before him . . . then Pharaoh transferred his ring . . . and set it on Joseph's hand. Esther 6:11, Berg's translation, reads, "and he arrayed . . . and had him ride . . . and he cried out before him . . . then the king transferred his ring . . . and gave it to Mordecai." There are many similar examples. Both tales feature Jewish heroes who rise to power in a foreign land. The protagonists of both stories confront similar problems. Berg summarizes:

> "Some post-exilic Jews, particularly in the Diaspora . . . were interested in the new possibilities for rich and rewarding lives under the friendly rule of their Persian masters. . . . The story of Joseph and the Book of Esther relate the success of Jews at a foreign court. They perhaps represent common expressions of the aspirations of some post-exilic Jews. . . . Whether intended by Esther's author or not, the story's ancient audience undoubtedly was reminded of the earlier story."

Other biblical books share literary characteristics with the book of Esther. The book of Daniel, the book of Ruth, and the book of Jonah all feature examples of the kinds of problems that Jews face in the Diaspora. In some way,

Esther and Babylonian Myth

In the 19th and early 20th centuries, some Bible scholars came to believe that the story of Esther may have been rooted in ancient myths about deities from Mesopotamia and the Near East. The names Mordecai and Esther sound a bit like those of the Babylonian deities Marduk and Ishtar. Vashti and Haman are names connected to the gods of Elam, an ancient nation conquered by the Persians. As a result, these scholars theorized that the story of Esther might have originated with a tale about the competitive nature of Elamite and Babylonian gods, with the Babylonian gods becoming the victors.

Today, most scholars reject this viewpoint. Scholar Michael V. Fox notes that it is perfectly reasonable to assume that an exiled people would, after time, give their children regional-sounding names.

Detail of a lion from the Ishtar Gate, one of the enormous entrances to the city of Babylon. Although the book of Esther dates the origins of Purim to the fifth century B.C.E., some scholars believe that Jews began celebrating the festival during the Babylonian captivity.

each book illustrates what it takes for a Jew to survive in a foreign empire. The apocryphal book of Judith also shares many characteristics of the Esther story. Judith and Esther are both beautiful women who rise to power from a lower station in life. The biggest difference is that in Judith, Daniel, and the other books the hand of God is more readily seen. In Esther, God's presence is hidden—if indeed He is there at all.

Many scholars—including Adele Berlin, Carol Bechtel, and Carey Moore—point to the comic, exaggerated features of the Esther story. Berlin calls the book of Esther a "burlesque," a farcical treatment that mocks the Persian Empire, peopling it with inept, even deranged, individuals who are incapable of doing their jobs properly. Another characteristic of burlesque literature is the false dignity and importance it gives to unimportant matters. For example, when Queen Vashti refuses to obey her husband, not only does the king remove her, but, at the suggestion of his attendants, issues an imperial decree that "all wives will honor their husbands. . . . every man should be lord in his own home" (Esther 1:20–21). Scholars agree the King of Persia probably would not issue an empire-wide decree of this nature simply because he couldn't control his wife.

GENRE

Pinning down the genre of the book of Esther, if it is not actual history, is difficult, even for the scholars. Berlin's position is that the book is intentional comedy; Carey Moore holds it to be historical fiction based in legend. Michael Fox rejects that it is Wisdom literature (like Proverbs, Ecclesiastes, or Job) or simply a fictitious story from the Persian court. He rules out historical novella/romance as a genre, saying it lacks "the romance's favorite themes and motifs: sudden and overpowering passions, heavy sentimentality, swooning, separation and reunion, chastity under temptation, and religion—cults, prayers, oracles, and divine interventions."

Fox is comfortable calling the book of Esther a story that depicts Jewish life in the Diaspora. He also terms it history in the sense that the author intended to convey a true historical reality—the threat to the survival of the Jewish people, and their religion and culture, in foreign lands—in an imaginative way. Fox writes of his own experience hearing the scroll read:

> "Although I doubt the historicity of the Esther story . . . every year at Purim when I hear the Scroll read in the synagogue, I know that it is true, whatever the historical accuracy of its details. Indeed, I relive its truth and know its actuality. Almost without an effort of imagination, I feel something of the anxiety that seized the Jews of Persia upon learning of Haman's threat to their lives, and I join in their exhilaration at their deliverance. Except that I do not think 'their', but 'my.'"

The memorable story in the book of Esther is dear to the Jews because it acts out in dramatic form an experience they claim individually and as a people. The story shows how Jews have endured bad treatment and emerged victorious, and assures them they shall continue to do so.

IN SEARCH OF A QUEEN

The story of Esther and her glorious rise to wealth and status begins without her presence. Depending on the version, one to two years pass before Esther comes into the action; and years transpire before she takes the initiatives for which she is remembered today: saving her people from destruction.

According to Addition A, one of the sections added in the Septuagint text, the story begins in the second year of the reign of Ahasuerus, king of Persia. Mordecai, an exiled Jew living in Susa, serves in the king's court. He has a troubling dream:

> There was noise and tumult, thunder and earthquake—confusion upon the earth. Two great dragons came on, both poised for combat. They uttered a mighty cry, and at their cry every nation prepared for war, to fight against the race of the just. It was a dark and gloomy day. Tribulation and distress, evil

and great confusion, lay upon the earth. The whole race of the just were dismayed with fear of the evils to come upon them, and were at the point of destruction. Then they cried out to God, and as they cried, there appeared to come forth a great river, a flood of water from a little spring. The light of the sun broke forth; the lowly were exalted and they devoured the nobles. (Catholic Bible Publishers: The New American Bible, 1987; Esther A:4–10).

Mordecai is puzzled by this dream and tries to understand its meaning. He continues in his palace position, most likely in a job at the king's gate. Mordecai eventually learns that two palace guards, Bagathan and Thares, have hatched a plot to kill Ahasuerus. He informs the king. After investigating the matter and gaining a confession from the traitors, Ahasuerus puts the eunuchs to death. The king then rewards Mordecai with a position of importance in the royal court.

Haman the Agagite—soon to be revealed as the villain of this story—already holds a position of honor in Persia.

> Jewish legends are tales that have been told over the centuries but that do not come directly from the Tanakh, or Jewish Bible. They are often derived from the Talmud (an authoritative collection of Jewish laws and legal decisions, along with commentary) and the Midrash (stories that expand on Bible incidents, to illustrate legal or moral principles). Rabbis often used the Midrash to fill in gaps in the Torah (the first five books of the Tanakh). These collective stories are also called *Haggadah*, the Hebrew word for legends of the Bible.

He is not pleased that the eunuch-guards have been executed, and decides to find a way to harm Mordecai.

This addition to the Septuagint, found in the Roman Catholic version of the book of Esther, serves many functions. It is a prologue to the Hebrew version, introducing Mordecai and indicating his position in the king's court. It details Mordecai's genealogy (repeated in Esther 2:5, 6). It introduces Haman and gives a reason for his future hatred of Mordecai: there is a strong implication that Haman had been involved in the eunuchs' plot to dispose of the king. Palace intrigue will play a role in this story.

But more than anything, Addition A proclaims God's presence and control in the tale. God's name is mentioned twice in this addition, although it is never mentioned in the entire Masoretic version of the story.

The Addition, with its dream of earthquake and tumult, also gives an apocalyptic slant to the story, similar to the tone of the book of Daniel. Apocalyptic literature originated in the years following the return of the exiled Jews from Babylon. It was concerned with visions and symbolism. Old Testament scholar Bernhard Anderson writes, "The central theme of the apocalyptic literature is God's revelation concerning the end time, the coming of the Kingdom of God. . . . Israel understood that her life was involved in a great drama which, under the direction of God, was moving toward a final consummation."

The story of Esther was probably written in the post-exilic age. This was a time when Jews lived under the rule of great empires—first Persian, and later Greek—and often faced great persecution. It would be natural for the author or editor of the Esther scroll to incorporate apocalyptic elements common to the literature of the time in order to bring a sense of God's involvement and to offer hope for the future.

A Party in the Capital

The Masoretic text begins the story a year after the events described in Addition A—the third year in the reign of King Ahasuerus of Persia, whose kingdom stretches from India to Ethiopia. At the palace stronghold of Susa, the king is giving a banquet for the officers and ministers of his kingdom. The Persian and Median aristocracy are there, and the king's army chiefs of staff, not to mention the nobles and governors of the one hundred twenty-seven provinces. The party lasts one hundred eighty days, enough time for the king to display the glorious riches and resplendent wealth of his kingdom (Esther 1:1–4). The party, according to scholars, might be to commemorate Ahasuerus's marriage to Vashti, or to celebrate his birthday, or to celebrate the building of a new capital.

Rabbis who contributed to the Midrash, a collection of stories and legends about Biblical characters, speculate that Ahasuerus may be celebrating the crushing of a rebellion (perhaps related to the eunuchs' plot described in Addition A); or, he may be attempting to win over the political heads of his kingdom to prevent future assassination attempts. These legends note, also, the king's disdain for the Jews, saying that he used Temple vessels for wine and even dressed in the robes of the high priest.

The Historical Xerxes

Ahasuerus (in Hebrew, Ahashwerosh) is a character patterned after the historical Persian shah Kyshayarsha; in English, this ruler is usually called Xerxes. Most scholars acknowledge that Ahasuerus in the book of Esther is Xerxes in name only. He possesses some of the traits attributed to the historical Xerxes, but is portrayed as something of a buffoon, according to scholars like Fox and Berlin. The author of the Esther story uses Xerxes to

Bas-relief depicting Persian courtiers, from the remains of a building at Persepolis. The father of Xerxes, Darius I (ruled 549 to 486 B.C.E.) had begun construction of this capital city; much of the work was completed during Xerxes's reign.

place the story in historical context to identify the origin of Purim, an existing festival, but at the same time to make fun of the empire that ruled over the Jews. Noting that Purim is a fun-filled, carnival-like holiday, Adele Berlin maintains that the story of its origin should not be taken too seriously:

> Chapter 1 [of Esther] sets the tone of the book, and it is a tone of excess, buffoonery, and bawdiness. It portrays the Persian court in all its decadent lavishness, and, with a hint of mockery so at home in burlesque, it paints a picture of a bumbling king and his overly ambitious courtiers.

The real Xerxes ruled the Persian Empire from 485 B.C.E. until he was assassinated in 465 B.C.E. Most historians of that time remember him with respect, but are quick to point out that although he ruled an empire stretching from India to Nubia, he never conquered the Greeks and, so, never ruled the East. Though he managed to approach Athens, his armies were badly beaten in the Battle of Salamis (479 B.C.E.). Adele Berlin writes,

> In Greek sources, Xerxes is portrayed as cruel, corrupt, and decadent; he is the image of the Asiatic despot as he ushers in the decline of the Persian empire. It is no accident, of course, that the Greeks portrayed him in this way, for he was the king who fought against Greece in an unsuccessful attempt to conquer it. The Greek attitude toward Xerxes is complex and ambivalent: he is the enemy and 'the other,' representing a culture antithetical to Greek culture; at the same time his is a worthy opponent, master of a world empire, and there is a certain fascination with him and his court.

The Persian Empire under Xerxes was highly organized, with twenty to thirty regions called satrapies subdivided into districts (provinces), each with governmental heads, called satraps. Roads connected all ends of the Empire, and a relay messaging system using horses and riders (similar to the Pony Express of American history) carried important messages across the realm. The Persians remained in power until the rise of Alexander the Great in 333 B.C.E.

THE CAPITAL CITY ON A HILL

Susa (Shushan), the citadel serving as the setting for the biblical story, was one of four capitals used by the Persian king at various times of the year; Susa was the winter residence, actually a fortress (acropolis) with a city below, the two being separated by a canal. The other cities were Ecbatana, Babylon, and Persepolis. Susa, once the capital of Elam, was chosen by Darius I, Xerxes' father, as the administrative capital of the empire. Darius undertook great building projects there.

Archaeology has provided much corroborating information to the biblical description of the grand palace at

The Persian Empire

Around 576 B.C.E., a king named Kurash (in English, Cyrus) appeared on the historical stage in ancient Persia. Under Cyrus, great conquests enlarged the Persian empire. Asia Minor, Croesus, the Babylonian empire, and much of the ancient world from the eastern Mediterranean to Central Asia were brought under control of Persian kings.

Cyrus the Great was the first of the line of the Persian rulers known as the Achaemenid dynasty. This name comes from one of Cyrus's ancestors, a man named Achaemenes.

After Cyrus's death in 529 B.C.E., his son Cambyses conquered Egypt. After a brief period of governmental instability, Darius I gained the Persian throne in 522 B.C.E. Early in his rule, Darius was mostly concerned with putting down revolts in the empire; he also expanded Persian rule into the European region known as the Caucasus.

The Persians had a formidable army. However, under Darius's son and successor Xerxes, Persia failed in an attempt to conquer the Greek city-states, such as Sparta and Athens (480–479 B.C.E.). The Persians and Greeks would wage war periodically over the next 150 years. Ultimately, the Macedonian ruler Alexander the Great conquered the Persian Empire in 331 B.C.E., bringing the Achaemenid dynasty to an end.

Susa—a kind of description rare in the Bible, and more in tune with descriptions written in Greek romances, or in apocryphal material such as in the book of Judith. The palace, courtyards, and gardens were a showpiece for the royal city. Adele Berlin reports that "inscriptions on tablets deposited in the foundation of Darius's palace buildings describe its construction and record the importation of materials (expensive woods, precious stones, gold, silver, ivory and ebony) and skilled craftsmen from all parts of the empire." Little of Susa's grandeur remains today because so much of the building material was wood and mud brick instead of stone.

The palace at Persepolis, built by Xerxes in the last thirteen years of his reign, was dedicated to Ahuramazda, the god of Zoroastrianism, and to Xerxes himself. Today, the ruins of Persepolis bear testimony to the staggering wealth of the Persians—a monument to their love of art and majestic structures. The king had residences in all of his capital cities. No price was too high to prevent him from living in the most lavish circumstances. Little wonder Ahasuerus needed six months to adequately share his glorious kingdom with his closest officers and political associates. In *The*

Carved figure of a griffin, a mythological beast with the body of a lion and the head of an eagle, from the palace at Persepolis. In ancient Persia, the griffin was considered a symbol of divine authority as well as a guardian of royal wealth.

This small silver statuette from the court of Artaxerxes I (464–424 B.C.E.) depicts a dignitary dressed in Persian trousers and Kyrbasia cap.

Legends of the Jews, a collection of Midrash and folklore by Jewish scholar Louis Ginzberg, he notes that "The splendor . . . is the gauge whereby to measure the wealth and power [Esther] enjoyed."

THE FOLLOW-UP PARTY

Not content with a party only six months in duration, the first feast (literally in Hebrew, *mishteh*, "drinking") winds down, and Ahasuerus invites the locals who live in the palace stronghold to a much simpler, scaled down party of only seven days, to be held in the palace's garden court. This site, too, has been specially prepared, according to the description in Esther 1: "There were white cotton draperies and violet hangings, held by cords of crimson bysus from silver rings on marble pillars. Gold and silver couches were on the pavement, which was of porphyry, marble, mother-of-pearl, and colored stones. Liquor was served in a variety of golden cups, and the royal wine flowed freely, as befitted the king's munificence" (Esther 1:6–7). Ginzberg's account adds additional details: "the upper branches of the high trees were made to interlace with each other, so as to form vaulted arches, and the smaller trees with aromatic foliage were taken up out of the ground, and placed in artfully constructed tents." Rules of order usually stated guests could only drink when the king drank, but Ahasuerus has thrown out this formality; attendees at this banquet are encouraged to drink as much as, and whenever, they wish! This feast is like a modern reception, with people able to come and go as

The Greek historian Herodotus noted the Persians' fondness for wine: "If an important decision is to be made, they discuss the question when they are drunk, and the following day the master of the house where the discussion was held submits their decision for reconsideration when they are sober. If they still approve it, it is adopted; if not, it is abandoned. Conversely, any decision they make when they are sober, is reconsidered afterwards when they are drunk." Herodotus, who lived during the time Persia and Greece were at war, is understandably insulting in his remarks.

they please—a kind of ancient lawn party, since the area of the palace where it was held could not accommodate the entire population at one sitting.

Louis Ginzberg, retelling Jewish legends, credits the villainous Haman for organizing the celebrations at Susa, and says they were meant to turn God against the Jewish people. "Their God," says Haman to Ahasuerus, "hates an unchaste life. Do thou, therefore, prepare feast for them, and order them to take part in the merry-makings. Have them eat and drink and act as their heart desireth, so that their God may become wrathful against them."

Queen Vashti's Defiance

Queen Vashti, perhaps knowing the lawn party had already or would soon degenerate into a males-only drinking bash, holds a party of her own elsewhere in the palace for the women. The rabbinic account notes that Vashti's party was every bit as nice as her husband's (but certainly more sedate and cultured), serving the women with fine meats, wines, liqueurs, and sweets. Vashti's guests lounged in the beautiful palace chambers and toured the magnificent interior spaces. Vashti, of course, knew how to win over these women whose drunken husbands were even then clamoring for something more than good food and conversation—a fact she would soon realize.

Seven days into the party, Ahasuerus, well under the influence of wine, merrily sends his seven eunuch attendants to "bring Queen Vashti into his presence wearing the royal crown, that he might display her beauty to the populace and the officials, for she was lovely to behold" (Esther 10–11). Though scholars disagree, a Midrash claims that Ahasuerus summoned Vashti to parade in front of the crowd wearing only her crown—that is, stark naked. Ahasuerus, it seems, hoped to exhibit his wife's charms, comparing her against women of Persia and Media, the wives of the men in attendance. The rabbis state that Vashti earned this invitation because of her bad treatment of Jewish servant maidens; according to this legend, the queen had forced them to spin and weave on the Sabbath, wearing nothing at all.

It would be a serious offense for anyone to refuse the command of a Persian king—even his wife. Anyone could and would be punished, perhaps killed, for a lapse in protocol. But Vashti refuses to come to the party.

Persian women did dine with their husbands. But more than one ancient account reveals that once the meal was over, and the serious drinking was about to begin, the husbands sent the wives out, replacing them with dancing girls and concubines. Adele Berlin sums up the reason for Vashti's refusal: "Nice queens don't go to drinking parties." And this party was already a week old.

A Not-So-Powerful King

Ahasuerus has a fit at his wife's refusal; the biblical account says, "the king's wrath flared up, and he burned with fury (Esther 1:12b). He calls in his seven law advisors and asks what he can legally do with the Queen because of her disobedience.

Memucan, the king's lead advisor, evades the legal question, and instead indicates to Ahasuerus that Queen Vashti's conduct has wronged not only the king, but also all the officials and populace of the province. Soon, all women in the kingdom will learn of Vashti's disobedience toward her husband and will pattern themselves after her bad example—there will be rebellion in the kingdom! The only way to deal with Vashti, Memucan continues, is to make an example of her by replacing her with another queen, and by forbidding Vashti to ever again enter the king's presence. Then, the king must issue "an irrevocable royal decree" (Esther 1:19) to that effect, and enter it into the laws of the Persians and the Medes.

The king accepts the advice, and sends letters to "all the royal provinces, to each province in it own script and to each people in its own language . . . that every man should be lord in his own home" (Esther 1:22). The Persian message relay system delivers the edict. The biblical account is silent about the fate of Vashti. She is never mentioned again; the rabbinic Midrash speculates that Ahasuerus has her executed.

Modern commentators point out the humor in Ahasuerus's need to consult his advisors and write new laws in order to control and punish his wife. The great and powerful Persian ruler is unable to solve a simple domestic dispute, and his top advisors and strategists seem to lack stability. The self-proclaimed "King of Kings," the builder of cities and palaces, cannot be, as Fox says, the king in this story, "the weak and unsteady despot [who] cannot be expected to care about anything besides his own pride and pleasure."

"In short," adds Carol Bechtel, "Ahasuerus may be a buffoon . . . but he is a dangerous buffoon"—dangerous because he is all too willing to place his tremendous power into the hands of his underlings. Esther and Mordecai, waiting to enter the story, will learn that fact all too well.

CHEERING UP THE KING

After this, the book of Esther describes Ahasuerus thinking back on past events, perhaps seeing them more clearly once his anger subsided. Some scholars suggest the king thinks back on Vashti with affection, perhaps regretting what has happened; he may wish there was a way of countermanding his own irrevocable decree.

The young men, his personal attendants who serve him in his chamber, have a plan to cheer him up. It is so simple a plan it is surprising that Ahasuerus doesn't think of it himself; but, many commentators point out that in this story the king does not have many original thoughts. Most of his ideas are put into his head by someone else. The king's young advisors suggest that all the young women should be brought to the palace. These virgins shall receive cosmetic treatments, rubbings with exotic oils, for a year. Once readied, they will be rotated through the king's bedchamber until he selects the one that pleases him the most. Then they will all remain in the harem safe and sound. The plan pleases Ahasuerus and he gives the command to make it so.

MORDECAI AND ESTHER

Meanwhile, in another part of the city live a Jewish man named Mordecai and his young cousin Esther. Mordecai is of the tribe of Benjamin, and is descended from people taken into exile from Jerusalem in 586 B.C.E. He is a foster father to Esther; her father's death had occurred before her birth, and her mother died while giving birth to her, says the Jewish legends.

According to the legends, Mordecai kept Esther hidden in a room so that she would not be discovered during Ahasuerus's queen candidate search. However, his neighbors knew about her beauty, so the king's scouts reported to the king that the most beautiful of all the women had eluded capture. "Thereupon Ahasuerus issued a decree ordaining the death penalty for the woman who should secrete herself before his emissaries," writes Ginzberg. "There was nothing left for Mordecai to do but fetch Esther from her hiding place, and immediately she was espied and carried to the palace of the king."

TO THE HAREM!

Esther is brought to the royal harem, the collection of virgins being prepared to become the king's bedmates. Esther catches the eye of Hegai, the eunuch who oversees the harem, and he favors her and makes sure that she has special attendants of her own.

At Mordecai's insistence, Esther keeps her Jewish identity a secret. This might indicate that there was some ill-feeling toward Jews in Persia. It might also be a literary technique of the author; certain Greek stories of the time included hidden identities as part of their plot.

Each day, Mordecai would walk in front of the harem's court to check on her safety and condition. Scholars seem to agree that Mordecai probably held some minor position in the palace at this juncture of the story, so it would not seem unusual for him to be present at the harem's doorway. Michael Fox notes that "if one pictures the Persian palace as a large, bustling compound that allows opportunities for discreet inquiries facilitated by bribes to maids and eunuchs, who would maintain discretion or hazard loss of future revenue," then it is easy to accept the plausibility of Mordecai's watchful presence.

After the twelve months of required preparation—six month's rubbing with oil of myrrh, and six months with

---

Harems were an expression of wealth and power, involving the total submission of hundreds of women to the whims of the king. Harems were common to biblical kings; even David and Solomon had wives and concubines. Multiple marriages often helped strengthen alliances between nations.

perfumes and cosmetics—each girl would take something of her choice from the harem when she was summoned to the king's bed. In the morning, she would join a second harem, a virgin no more; now she was watched over by Shaashgaz and had a new descriptor: concubine. The girl would remain in the second harem unless the king remembered her well enough to call her back by name.

Being part of the king's harem is not necessarily fun for those involved. Carol Bechtel points out that the young women do not choose to be there. "There are no parting gifts [for those not selected]," Bechtel writes, "and they do not get to go home. They go straight into the harem . . . a poor substitute for freedom, home, and family."

Esther's Turn

Esther's time finally comes, and she goes to the king, taking with her some unnamed item suggested by Hegai. It was then the seventh year of Ahasuerus's reign, four years after the banquets that opened the story. Hegai's advice and Esther's beauty win the day, and the king loves her best of all. He places the crown on her head and makes her queen, following up with another great feast in her honor, giving gifts and a time of tax relief in the provinces. There is a great positive feeling about the new queen. The citizens welcome parties and tax cuts with enthusiasm.

Although she is queen, Esther continues to hide her Jewish identity. The Midrash suggests that Mordecai's modesty might have been part of the reason: he doesn't want any special favors from the king just because his relative is queen. The rabbis also write that because so much hatred existed toward the Jews, Mordecai feared that Esther would suffer the same fate as Vashti.

The final verses of Esther 2 seem almost an afterthought, but an important one; they set up a coincidence that will occur later in the story. Mordecai is stationed at the king's gate, where he overhears a conversation between two eunuch guards, Bagathan and Thares, who are angrily plotting to kill Ahasuerus. In the Masoretic version, the assassination plot does not involve Haman, as is implied in Addition A of the Septuagint. Mordecai happens to be in the right place at the right time, and he lets

Servants prepare the Jewish maiden Esther to meet the Persian king. Esther 2:7 describes her as "beautifully formed and lovely to behold."

The coronation of Esther as queen of Persia: "Now the king was attracted to Esther more than to any of the other women, and she won his favor and approval.... So he set a royal crown on her head and made her queen instead of Vashti. And the king gave a great banquet, Esther's banquet, for all his nobles and officials. He proclaimed a holiday throughout the provinces and distributed gifts with royal liberality" (Esther 2:17–18).

Esther know about the plan. She tells the king, who investigates, learns the truth of the matter, and has the men impaled and hung on a gibbet (essentially run through with a wooden stake and placed, skewered, upright in the ground—a punishment meant to deter anyone with similar ideas). The event is recorded in the king's official history and tucked away on a shelf. But it will surface again.

Much in this story "comes around again," thanks to skillful use by the author of repetition, reversals, and irony. For now, the preliminaries are completed and the main characters have been introduced, save for one. He is the personification of evil, poised to walk on stage.

Haman's Revenge

Haman is the villain of the story in the book of Esther—vile, scheming, and murderous. He appears out of nowhere in the Hebrew version, elevated by Ahasuerus to a position of power shortly after the attempt on the king's life. Haman is a man of some influence, and he is rich beyond imagining.

Almost from the beginning, in a very few verses, Haman's intent to bring destruction and disorder is clear. He is far cleverer than Ahasuerus, who is preoccupied with his parties and his harem, and who has shown himself incapable of making even the simplest decisions. Driven by jealousy and an unquenchable thirst for power, Haman easily brings his insidious plan into being.

Haman had made his first appearance in the rabbinic commentary during the king's second banquet in Esther 1. There he was busy making the Jewish guests embarrassed before their God, placing them at a raucous party scene, tempting them to gluttony and drunkenness; it is clear Haman has an agenda against the Jews. At this juncture of the story, the scholarly commentary implies Ahasuerus, too, may at least discriminate against them. Though Mordecai, the Jew, has just saved Ahasuerus from certain death at the hands of two plotting eunuch-guards, Haman is the one chosen to become grand vizier, second in command to the king. Haman is the son of Hammedatha the Agagite, a descendant of King Agag of the Amalekites.

HISTORICAL BASIS FOR HATRED

The Amalekites had troubled Israel as far back as the time of the Exodus from Egypt and the forty years of wilderness wandering, until the days of Saul. In I Samuel 15, the prophet Samuel anoints Saul king over Israel and commissions him to punish Agag and his people. Samuel commands Saul to utterly destroy them and everything they have. Saul and his army of thousands confront the Amalekites, and defeat and destroy them. But contrary to God's command, Saul does not destroy the best of the animals, nor does he destroy King Agag; he claims he plans to sacrifice the animals to the Lord; he does not say what he plans to do with Agag.

Yahweh speaks to Samuel, and reveals how Saul disobeyed. Obeying the Lord is more important than sacrifice. Yahweh regrets he ever made Saul king and sends Samuel to give Saul the news. Saul begs for mercy, but Samuel shuns him and sends for Agag. Agag swaggers in, smiling, and Samuel, the great prophet of God, takes a sword and hacks Agag to pieces. Saul's mishandling of God's directive costs him his kingship. The descendants of Saul bear a grudge against Agag's line, identifying Agag as the reason for Saul's fall from God's grace.

Haman's Revenge

Illustration from a 17th century Persian manuscript that depicts the Israelites and Amalekites in battle. Conflict between these two ancient peoples apparently began when the Israelites were fleeing from Egypt; in Deuteronomy 25:17–18 Moses reminds the people, "Remember what Amalek did to you on the way as you came out of Egypt, how he attacked you on the way when you were faint and weary, and cut off your tail, those who were lagging behind you, and he did not fear God." After another battle described in Exodus, God tells Moses, "I will completely blot out the memory of Amalek from under heaven." During the Purim celebration, Jews participating in the reading of Esther make noise each time Haman's name appears, so that it is "blotted out" and cannot be heard.

Saul is a Benjamite, a descendant of Benjamin, son of the patriarch Jacob; Mordecai is a Benjamite as well, making Mordecai and Saul kinsmen. Haman, an Agagite, is a descendant of Agag. So, in view of the occurrence described in I Samuel 15, a generations-old blood feud exists between them. Ahasuerus the king announces that all the king's servants must bow to Haman, who has been lifted higher in rank than the rest of them. While the king's staff bows low, Mordecai stands his ground. The servants are amazed and shocked; they remind Mordecai of this new requirement, but Mordecai states that he is a Jew. They rush to Haman and tell him, wanting to know if Mordecai's explanation is acceptable. Interestingly, say the scholars, Haman hasn't noticed Mordecai standing there; he is so egotistical, so full of conceit and bloated self-importance, that others have to tell him Mordecai is disobeying the rules.

WHY WON'T MORDECAI BOW DOWN?

Commentators speculate about Mordecai's refusal to comply with the king's law. Was he angry he had not been rewarded with a promotion for saving the king's life? Is he simply stubborn or arrogant? As a Jew, is he refusing to bow before another human being, saving that level of reverence for God? Some commentators, searching for a "God connection" in the story suggest this, especially on the basis of Mordecai's prayer in the Septuagint's Addition C. There Mordecai prays, "But I acted as I did so as not to place the honor of man above that of God" (Esther Addition C: verse 7).

The rabbis supposed Haman wore the image of an idol fastened to his clothes, so Mordecai, a good Jew, refused to bow to Haman and thereby bow to the idol at the same time. The rabbis work hard to develop the religious connection so lacking in the Hebrew text, putting strong words in Mordecai's mouth:

> Before such [a] one I should prostrate myself? I bend the knee before God alone, the only living One in heaven, He who is the fire consuming all other fires; who holds the earth in His arms; who stretches out the heavens in His might; who darkens the sun when it pleases Him, and illumines the darkness.... To Him praise is due, before Him we must prostrate ourselves.

Ginzberg relates another legend of a long-standing secret Mordecai held against Haman. Mordecai once helped Haman out of a difficulty and required, as payment, Haman sell himself to Mordecai as a slave. Haman complied, and the bill of sale was recorded on Mordecai's kneecap. Once Haman received his high rank in the court of Ahasuerus, Mordecai frequently showed him his kneecap to remind him of their bargain. This infuriated Haman, and he swore vengeance.

Michael Fox refutes these ideas, however, instead identifying "tribal enmity" as the explanation. "Mordecai refuses to bow because he will not humble himself before a scion of Israel's archetypal enemy." A Benjamite will not grovel before a descendant of Agag. His explanation: "I am a Jew" is reason enough.

When Haman learns that Mordecai refuses to bow down, he is filled with the same kind of rage (*hemah*) exhibited by Ahasuerus when Vashti would not display herself before the partygoers. Carol Bechtel points to the disproportionate actions in the book of Esther, the tendency to over- or underreact. Vashti's refusal brings a kingly edict upon all women (submit to your husbands!). Haman's rage has the same effect. It will not be enough to punish Mordecai alone. Not only will Mordecai "have hands laid on him" (be killed), but so will all Jews in the realm.

THE PLAN IS BORN

Haman's arrogance is so complete, his ego so inflated, he proceeds with his plan to find a suitable date upon which to slaughter Mordecai and the rest of the Jews before getting the king's permission. Using the time-honored tradition of casting a *pur* (a lot or stone die, from the Old Babylonian *puru*, "fate."), Haman calls on his diviners to conjure up a date.

The lot is cast in the first month, Nisan, a time when the gods were setting out the events of the year. The date of the destruction will be the thirteenth day of the twelfth month, Adar. Interpreters explain the eleven-month delay as a dramatic technique of the author, giving Mordecai and Esther time to save their people.

Next, Haman needs to convince the king that the Persian Jews need to be wiped off the face of the earth. Haman's case is simple—simple enough for a simpleton king willing to let everyone else do his thinking for him. It is a position based on half-truths and outright lies. "Dispersed among the nations throughout the provinces of your kingdom, there is a certain people living apart, with laws differing from those of every other people," he

> Proverbs 16:33 infers that when lots are cast, God—not random chance—determines the outcomes. "The lot is cast into the lap, but its every decision is from the Lord."

Haman speaks to Ahasuerus, offering an enormous bribe if he will permit the destruction of the Jews in Persia. The 10,000 silver talents would weigh about 345 metric tons; at the current price of silver (about $11.25 an ounce), the value of Haman's bribe is staggering: nearly $137 million!

tells Ahasuerus. "They do not obey the laws of the king, and so it is not proper for the king to tolerate them. If it please the king, let a decree be issued to destroy them; and I will deliver to the procurators ten thousand silver talents for deposit in the royal treasury" (Esther 3:8–9).

True, the Jews are dispersed, spread throughout the kingdom; Haman gives a mysterious twist to this irrelevant fact by failing to name exactly who the "certain people" are. Michael Fox comments, "The Jews were not the only exiled people dispersed in the former Babylonian empire. But in the context of the accusation, 'scattered' insinuates moral disintegration and lack of substance, as well as insidious ubiquity: this unnamed people is all around you." Their "different laws" would have been laws of Jewish practice, such as eating kosher food, observing religious festivals, manners of speech or dress—nothing of any real threat to the kingdom, though Haman makes it seem so.

In *Legends of the Jews*, Haman condemns the Jews by name, listing all their religious activity through the year, both on special festival days and throughout each day, taking time to fast, or pray, or to assemble as a people of their God. "In this way they waste the whole year with tomfoolery and fiddle-faddle, only in order to avoid doing the king's service," Haman tells Ahasuerus.

Perhaps feeling he has not fully condemned the Jews, Haman adds an indictment that they do not obey the laws of the king, that is, the imperial laws of the Persian Empire. This might refer to Mordecai's failure to bow down before Haman, as the king had commanded. Adele Berlin writes:

> In Ezra 4:12–16 it is claimed that the Jews returning to Judah will not pay tribute or taxes and that this will constitute sedition against the Persian king. In an inscription from Persepolis, the Persian King Xerxes invokes tribute and imperial law as the sign of his suzerainty: 'These are the countries . . . over which I hold sway . . . which are bringing their tribute to me . . . and they abide by my laws'

(Pritchard, *Ancient Near Eastern Texts*, 316). The author of Esther has put into Haman's mouth exactly the elements that constitute treason against the Persian king."

In case Ahasuerus hasn't quite made up his mind, Haman presents him with added incentive. He offers an enormous amount of money—by some accounts, 10,000 silver talents is equivalent to two-thirds the size of the empire's treasury—to sweeten and seal the deal. The money may come from Haman's private funds (the rabbis considered him wealthy), or perhaps from the value of goods that will be plundered from the soon-to-be-annihilated Jews; commentators disagree about the meaning intended by the passage. Clearly, Haman wants this deal to go through. Using his wealth as a manipulative tool has no doubt gotten Haman where he is today. For Haman to use his vast fortune for the good of others would be out of character.

Carol Bechtel comments on Sandra Beth Berg's research concerning the intended meaning of the Hebrew word "to destroy," an interesting linguistic puzzle. In speech, the Hebrew word for "destroy" sounds like the word for "rest," a word indicating an enslavement of the Jews, not their wholesale murder. Bechtel writes, "While it is obvious that [Haman] is a formidable enemy for the Jews, his considerable cunning may not be so obvious. That he could stoop to this kind of rhetorical trick—and hope to get away with it—catapults him into the category of evil genius." Perhaps Ahasuerus is fine with the plan because he believes he is enslaving the unknown people, not setting up a pogrom for their permanent removal.

Ahasuerus tells Haman to keep his money, and, handing him his signet ring, the official seal of the empire, he empowers this evil genius to work his will. "Do with them whatever you please," the king tells Haman (Esther 3:11). Once again, Ahasuerus is happy to let someone else worry about the details. In the Joseph account in Genesis 41:42, Pharaoh gives his signet ring to Joseph, elevating him to the status of ruler and allowing him to save his people. In the Esther story, Haman is about to use a king's signet ring to destroy the very same nation.

SEALING THE DEAL

All that remains now is to put the deal in writing, and Haman wastes no time. On the 13th of Nisan, the day before the Jewish Passover, Haman summons the scribes and dictates an edict, to be sent to the royal satraps, the governors, and the officials—duly translated into all the appropriate languages of the empire. Written in the name of Ahasuerus, sealed with the signet ring on Haman's own finger, it proclaimed that "all Jews, young and old, including women and children, should be killed, destroyed, wiped out in one day, the thirteenth day of the twelfth month, Adar, and that their goods should be seized as spoil" (Esther 3:13).

The Persian message-relay system was so efficient that the farthest provinces could be informed within three months—still leaving eight months to prepare the killing fields. Michael Fox writes,

> Haman's edict presumes that a great many people are waiting for the opportunity to destroy the Jews and need only be unleashed. The edict need not convince them to set to the task or explain why the Jews should be destroyed. In this we have hint that the conflict is not between two men alone, or even between two peoples within the empire, but between the Jews and masses of people through-

The Deadly Decree

Addition B of the Septuagint version of Esther includes the text of the royal edict sent to the Persian satraps and governors. Scholars feel that this Addition was originally composed in Greek (as was E); thus it is more recent than A, C, D, and F, which are all thought to be Hebrew in origin. The flowery, ornamental style of Addition B does not match the core accounts in Hebrew.

Though the edict is meant to sound as though it has been written by the king, it is clear from Esther 3:11–12 that Haman is the author. While the text opens with the king claiming his fair and humane approach to government, it quickly reverts to a focus on Haman, "who excels among us in wisdom, who is outstanding for constant devotion and steadfast loyalty, and who has gained the second rank in the kingdom" (Addition B.3). Haman's ego is inflated to the bursting point.

The letter identifies an unnamed people, bad willed, whose oppositional laws set them apart from law-abiding types, who prevent unity in the kingdom. They don't get along peaceably with anyone, live criminal lives, and create instability in the government. Haman has warmed to his position as king-substitute, "a second father" (Addition B:6) to all folk in the kingdom, their protector and benefactor. The letter gives enemies of the Jews license to kill them by the sword, along with their women and children. Whatever rhetorical trick Haman used to convince Ahasuerus in Esther 3:9, he makes sure to clarify that by "destroy" he means for the Jews to be killed, so that when they've gone down to the world of the dead they can no longer disrupt the affairs of the kingdom.

It is ironic that Haman sends his decree on the 13th of Nisan. The doom of the Jews in Persia seems assured on the day before the commemoration of Passover—a festival celebrating the Hebrews' deliverance from slavery in Egypt.

In Addition B, the 14th of Adar is identified as the day on which the Jews will be destroyed. Scholars are unclear as to why this varies from the Masoretic text, in which Haman gives the date of 13 Adar.

out the empire. Danger on a mass scale is always a reality for the Jews, but until a demagogue gives the hostility free rein, it stays fairly well in the background.

News of the impending slaughter leaks out to the city stronghold of Susa. Though most of the city of Susa recoils in horror, the rabbis in the Midrash, reported by Ginzberg, write, "The position of the Jews after the royal edict became known [begs] description. If a Jew ventured abroad on the street to make a purchase, he was almost throttled by the Persians, who taunted him with, 'Never mind, to-morrow will soon be here, and then I shall kill thee, and take thy money away from thee.'"

Haman and Ahasuerus have a *mishteh* (another drinking feast) to celebrate. For Haman, the best is yet to come; Ahasuerus is just enjoying a pleasant supper, unaware of the magnitude of his edict. For Mordecai and Esther, a call to action is at hand.

A Time to Mourn

Despite knowing that death has been predicted for the Jews, Mordecai takes the initiative to change the course of events. Mordecai has connections in the palace; it doesn't take him long to learn all the details of the plot. He reacts to the horrible news in a manner befitting a devout Jew of the time: he tears his clothing, puts on sackcloth, and, while walking around the city, cries aloud, throwing ashes on himself. Similar public expressions of grief can be found throughout the Bible. Commentators seeking God in the story of Esther typically interpret this behavior as the prayerful act of a religious man.

Although Mordecai's action may indicate deep religious faith, he may have had other reasons for his behavior. Mordecai may be feeling guilty because his failure to bow in homage before Haman has brought on the threat to the Jews. He may also want to bring the unjust nature of the

58 Esther

This 16th century Italian painting depicts Esther and her attendants in attire that would be appropriate at a Renaissance court, rather than a Persian palace.

edict to the attention of the citizens. Certainly he feels the grief of the entire Jewish population—"a great spasm of grief," as Bechtel puts it.

More than likely, though, Mordecai knows how to attract Esther's attention, and, since she is the queen, shock her into action. He winds his way through the streets until he reaches the king's gate at the palace. He can go no further, for sackcloth is considered improper attire there. All around, the Jews are described as being in deep mourning, with lamenting, sackcloth, ashes, and fasting, which is itself a form of prayer. However, scholars note that although the trappings of religious expression are evident, there is no direct outcry to God by name, nor is there a response from God. Adele Berlin writes,

> God is most present and most absent in this chapter. Religious practice and mention of God's name come closest to the surface here, and are most obviously suppressed. It is hard to read about fasting, mourning, and crying out without seeing God as the addressee to whom all these actions are directed. It is hard to plead for salvation from anyone but God. . . . That the comic nature of the book has prevented the mention of God is most evident now, when the book is least comic. In this sad scene, the author is hard pressed to write God out of the story.

ESTHER LEARNS OF THE PLOT

Queen Esther's eunuchs and maids tell her Mordecai is outside the palace gate in great distress and mourning. They somehow know of a connection between them; they may realize she, like he, is a Jew. It may be that the servants have been the link between Mordecai and Esther during his daily inquiries about her well-being in the harem. She sends him garments to replace the sackcloth so that he might enter and speak with her, but he refuses them.

Esther sends Hathach, one of the king's eunuchs in her service, to find out what is going on—she still has no idea. She has been in complete isolation in the harem. Mordecai tells Hathach everything, including the exact amount of silver Haman has offered to influence the king. Mordecai also gives Hathach a copy of the written decree.

Mordecai tells Hathach to send Esther to the King to plead for her people. Mordecai's request divulges Esther's Jewish identity, but Hathach may already know. The servants are friendly; they are more aware of inner palace dynamics than the royal family or a certain grand vizier. The secret is safe with them.

An additional verse (provided by the Septuagint) supplies what has been missing in the Hebrew text: "Invoke the Lord and speak to the king for us," says Mordecai; "save us from death" (Esther 4:9). Without that line, the Masoretic text places the responsibility for the salvation of a people on Mordecai and Esther alone. God's presence is missing.

Esther, through Hathach, reminds Mordecai of the grave danger of entering the presence of a king unbidden. Frequent political assassinations in the ancient Near East had led to strict measures of security. The historian Flavius Josephus, writing about Esther in his *Antiquities*, states, "Now the king had made a law, that none of his own people should approach him unless he were called, when he sat upon his throne, and men, with axes in their hands, stood around his throne, in order to punish such as approached to him without being called." If he extended the golden scepter toward the visitor, all would be well. If not, it meant certain death.

Esther is criticized in some of the older commentaries for hesitating to take action on behalf of her people because of the risk to her safety. But Adele Berlin feels it is all part of Esther's plan. "Esther is not refusing the task that Mordecai set before her; she is proposing a plan whereby it can be accomplished, and at the same time warning of the risk inherent in it. She risks losing her own life, which is not only a problem for her, but, more to the point of the dialogue, means that she would then be unable to plead for the Jews." Plus, Esther confesses, the king has not called for her in thirty days. Perhaps he will be overjoyed to see her; or, perhaps, he has developed an interest in others.

Mordecai's Warning

Upon receiving Esther's message, Mordecai counters with two more comments, acknowledged by many scholars to be allusions to God. He tells her not to think for a minute that she, being a Jew, will be safe from Haman's genocidal plot just because she lives in the palace. In fact, even if Esther remains silent, "relief and deliverance will come to the Jews from another source, but [Esther] and [Esther's father's] house shall perish" (Esther 4:14). And then, "Who knows but that it was for a time like this that you obtained the royal dignity?" (Esther 4:15). "Another source of rescue" implies a trust that God will take action

> In the story of Esther, palace officials take great pains to protect Ahasuerus the king from intruders who might harm him. Ironically, the historical Xerxes was murdered in his own bedroom by his uncle, Artabanus, and his grandson, Megabyzys.

to protect the Jews, His chosen people. Esther's presence in the palace may have been foreordained by God for a time such as they are experiencing.

GOD IN THE SHADOWS

Sandra Berg writes that "The narrator believed in a hidden causality behind the surface of human history, both concealing and governing the order and significance of events.... The Book of Esther, then, does not ignore the presence of divine activity; rather, it points to the hiddenness of Yahweh's presence in the world. Because Yahweh's control of history is neither overt nor easily discerned in everyday events, the determination of the shape and direction of history shifts to human beings."

This implied presence of God is the theological interpretation indicated by a number of modern scholars. But there are scholars who claim "another source of rescue" merely means "another human being." Michael Fox, for example, says that the Hebrew author of Esther is teaching a "theology of possibility:"

> This carefully crafted indeterminacy is best explained as an attempt to convey uncertainty about God's role in history. The author is not quite certain about God's role in these events and does not conceal that uncertainty.... The story's indeterminacy conveys the message that the Jews should not lose faith if they, too are uncertain about where God is in a crisis. Israel will survive—that is the author's faith—but how this will happen he does not know.... If anything is excluded, it is disbelief.

Esther sends back a message to Mordecai, and sounds every bit like a queen. Assemble all the Jews in Susa, she tells him, and fast for three entire days; she and her maids will do the same. Then she will go to the king, even if it means breaking the law, even if it means her death. And Mordecai obeys her, as once she had obeyed him. Mordecai fades out of the picture for a time; Esther's plan is about to take shape.

QUEEN ESTHER EMERGES

The Septuagint text incorporates two Additions at this point in the story. Addition C includes prayers by Mordecai and Esther, while Addition D tells of the reception of Esther into the King's chamber. This Addition replaces the first few verses of Chapter 5 in the Masoretic text. These additions provide evidence of God's continual presence and His control over events.

Mordecai's prayer is the prayer of a devout Jew, acknowledging God's power in the world. Mordecai says that he refused to bow to Haman so that he "would not place the honor of man above that of God" (C:7). He prays that God would deliver them from the certain death facing them. "Hear my prayer; have pity on your inheritance and turn our sorrow into joy: thus we shall live to sing praise to your name, O Lord" (C:10).

Esther removes her splendid garments and dons sackcloth. She covers her head with dirt and ashes; her body is adorned not with fine jewels, but with her tangled, filthy hair. Carol Bechtel quips, "One gets the impression that the effects of her yearlong beauty treatment have been undone in a matter of minutes." Her prayer is a great confession of God's faithful presence measured against the sins of the people. She prays for God's help in this time of trial for her people, and for herself, as she approaches the king. "Save us by your power, and help me, who am alone and have no one but you, O Lord" (C:25). She then confesses her hatred of life among the Persians—her abhorrence of her crown, of Haman, of the food and drink of the royal table, which are not ritually clean by any means. She hates being Queen of a Gentile court. She is appalled at sharing the bed of a Gentile king. She even claims to hate the glory, the wealth, of the pagans. Nothing, she prays, means more to her than Yahweh, the God of Abraham. "O God, more powerful than all, hear the voice of those in despair. Save us from the power of the wicked, and deliver me from my fear" (C:30).

Addition D finds Esther arrayed in her finest garments. According to legend, she was "arrayed . . . in a silken garment, embroidered with gold from Ophir and spangled with diamonds and pearls sent her from Africa; a golden crown was on her head, and on her feet shoes of gold." She approaches the king. Two maids support her, one at her arm, and one in control of the flowing train behind her. She is frightened, but exceedingly beautiful, as she enters the king's presence. He is dressed in his finest kingly attire, awesome to behold.

As their eyes meet, his face contorts with anger. This is too much for the frightened Esther to bear; she staggers as if to pass out. But God in that instant changes the king's anger to concern, and he leaps from the dais and catches her in his arms, reassuring her that she is safe. The king touches her with the golden scepter, imploring her to speak.

Ginzberg adds the rabbinic comment that "by reason of her long fast, Esther was so weak that she was unable to extend her hand toward the scepter of the king. The archangel Michael had to draw her near it." She tells the king she thought he was an angel, so astounding in his kingly array, and she passes out in his arms. Ahasuerus and his attendants are quite concerned and work to revive her.

Esther swoons before the Persian king, as described in the Septuagint version of the tale.

In the Septuagint text, God saves the day. But according to the Masoretic text, when Mordecai leaves the courtyard and Esther prepares to fast, there is no divine intercession. What Esther and Mordecai must do, they must do alone.

Dinner for Three

The Esther of the Masoretic text in chapter 5 is a different Esther than the one portrayed by Addition D to the Septuagint. This Esther does not require supportive maids; this Esther is not weak and fainting. Esther in the Hebrew Bible dresses in her royal garb and strides to the inner court, resolute to take action. Ready to perish if she must, she stands waiting until the king notices her—the Queen, awaiting audience with her husband. This Esther has a plan. And the plan does not involve seduction: she is dressed for a "royal business meeting," comments Adele Berlin.

Welcoming the Queen

Ahasuerus looks up and sees her, standing in her royal robes, calculated to remind the king Esther is not just another member of the harem. Weeks have passed since he has called for her; she wins his favor, just standing there, and he extends the golden scepter. He can see she is agitated. "What troubles you, Queen Esther? And what is your request? Even to half the kingdom, it shall be granted you" (Esther 5:3). The king realizes Esther has approached him at great peril to her life. As Carol Bechtel notes, "Dressing up to visit the king uninvited is a bit like venturing into a snake pit doing one's best imitation of a snake."

"If it please your majesty," Esther replies, "come today with Haman to a banquet I have prepared" (Esther 5:4). Bechtel points out that in the Hebrew, the invitation is to the king; the addition of Haman is an afterthought. "Let the king come—and Haman—today to the banquet that I have prepared for him." For Esther's plan to work, she needs Haman to attend. However, there will be no hesitation on Haman's part. It is a high honor to be invited to dine in private with the king and queen.

Commentators speculate about why Esther chooses to invite Haman. Perhaps she does so to lull him into a false sense of security. Perhaps it is to make the king jealous. Jewish legend recounts the scene with Esther unashamedly flirting with Haman during the banquet—moving her chair close to his, and allowing him to drink first out of the wine cup the king passes to her. Some scholars conclude she didn't want to be alone with the king that night; she didn't want the king getting the wrong idea about why he was invited to dinner. Seduction was not on the menu this evening.

Esther counts on Haman's ego swelling as he believes himself to be the center of attention. Of course, he *is* the center—but not in the way he thinks. The author's use of irony abounds. This banquet is a purposeful, calculated scheme. The trap is set. Ahasuerus loves parties—perhaps there will be wine! He sends servants to Haman to hurry him along to the banquet. The Queen has spoken.

DINNER WITH THE QUEEN

Ahasuerus and Haman enjoy the Queen's banquet, and, during the wine course at the end, the king asks again, "What does the Queen request?" With this question, the king offers his near iron-clad guarantee that her wish will be granted. Esther answers, "If I have found favor with the king and if it pleases your majesty to grant my petition and honor my request, come with Haman tomorrow to a banquet which I shall prepare for you; and then I will do as you ask"(Esther 5:8).

The drama builds. Has Esther lost her nerve? Does she feel the moment isn't right? Or is she playing the king (and Haman) like a master angler? Carey Moore writes "Postponing her real request another time was a most questionable gamble; any number of things could go wrong in the interval between the two dinners: the king's benevolent mood could change . . . or Haman could learn of Esther's true feelings toward him or of her relationship to Mordecai."

Another scholar notes how Ahasuerus is highly influenced by his advisors. If Haman learned the truth, or even imagined he knew the truth, he could take action against Esther. After all, the king disposed of Vashti quite handily at the suggestion of the king's advisors. How much more influential Haman would be as the grand vizier! But Ahasuerus has had too much wine, and Haman is too full of himself to see beyond the moment: they are going to dine again with the Queen—tomorrow! This time the dinner party invitation clearly includes Haman, but not as an afterthought. It is critical Haman attend the next party—to get his serving of just desserts.

Haman's Anger

Haman leaves the banquet happy and carefree, warm with wine and wonderment at this new respect shown him by the Queen. Ginzberg writes, "Haman felt secure in his position, priding himself not only on the love of the king, but also on the respect of the queen. He felt himself to be the most privileged being in all the wide realm governed by Ahasuerus." But his jovial mood dissipates when passing the

Renaissance-era painting of Esther hosting dinner for Ahasuerus and Haman.

king's gate. There at his post sits Mordecai, who no doubt glances up, makes eye contact with Haman, yawns, and goes about his business. Ginzberg records that Mordecai "pointed to his knee, inscribed with the bill of sale whereby Haman had become the slave of Mordecai. Doubly and triply enraged, [Haman] resolved to make an example of the Jew." Mordecai's action will incite instant retaliation on Haman's part. And, say the rabbis, Haman wouldn't be satisfied with just kicking Mordecai to death.

Haman slinks home, summoning his wife, Zeresh, and his friends. There he tells the people who know him best the wonderful achievements he has attained. He brags to them about his wealth. He reminds his wife and friends of his ten sons. In the ancient Near East, family size, especially the number of male offspring, signaled great achievement. Herodotus writes, "After prowess in fighting, the chief proof of manliness is to be the father of a large family of boys. Those who have most sons receive an annual present from the king—on the principle that there is strength in numbers."

Haman crows about how the king has promoted him and placed him above all the officials and royal servants in rank and importance. Plus, he has just returned from an exclusive dinner party with the royal couple, and is to attend another such banquet tomorrow. Queen Esther

Ruins of the so-called Xerxes Gate in Persepolis. In the Esther story, Haman is angry that his enemy Mordecai still has a position as the king's gate.

simply can't get enough of him! But every ounce of this glory is as nothing when he sees Mordecai the Jew, sitting at the palace gate.

Several commentators point out that Haman is angry about the fact Mordecai is sitting, not flat on the ground doing obeisance before the grand vizier. But he is also infuriated that Mordecai still has a job at the king's gate, such an important and powerful post. The Jewish legends say Haman points to a representation of his treasury chamber, inscribed on his breast, saying, "And all this is worthless in my sight when I look upon Mordecai, the Jew. What I eat and drink loses its savor, if I but think of him."

Zeresh and the advisors are quick to suggest a solution that will end Haman's agony a few months earlier than already planned. She hears the despair in his voice. According to a Jewish legend recorded by Louis Ginzberg, Zeresh says:

> If the man thou tellest of is a Jew, thou wilt not be able to do aught to him except by sagacity. If thou castest him into the fire, it will have no effect upon him, for Hananiah, Mishael, and Azariah [Shadrach, Meshak, and Abednego] escaped from the burning furnace unhurt; Joseph went free from prison; Manasseh prayed to God, and He heard him, and saved him from the iron furnace; to drive him out in the wilderness is useless, thou knowest the desert did not evil to the Israelites that passed through it; putting out his eyes avails naught, for Samson blind did more mischief than ever Samson seeing. Therefore hang him, for no Jew has ever escaped death by hanging."

She continues in the biblical account: "'Have a gibbet set up, fifty cubits in height, and in the morning ask the king to have Mordecai hanged on it. Then go to the banquet with the king in good cheer.' This suggestion pleased Haman, and he had the gibbet erected" (Esther 5:14).

The size of this gibbet is certainly an exaggeration. Fifty cubits is approximately 75 feet high, and would tower over everything in the city—if indeed it could be made to stand. No structure in the Bible is fifty cubits high, notes Adele Berlin. "Even Solomon's Temple is only thirty cubits high," Berlin writes. "Archaeologists estimate that the palaces of ancient capitals like Susa were perhaps forty to fifty feet high."

Preparing for Mordecai's Destruction

Once again, Haman makes his preparations before going to the king for permission. Ahasuerus, after all, has proven easy to convince; if the gibbet has already been erected, Haman can effect Mordecai's demise before the king has a change of heart. In the rabbinic commentary, Zeresh takes the lead in constructing the structure:

> She fetched artificers in wood and iron, the former to erect the cross, the latter to make the nails. Their children danced around in high glee while Zeresh played upon the cithern, and Haman in his pleasurable excitement said: "To the wood workers I shall give abundant pay, and the iron workers I shall invite to a banquet." When the cross was finished, Haman himself tested it, to see that all was in working order. A heavenly voice was heard: "It is good for Haman the villain, and for the son of Hammedatha it is fitting."

If Haman gets his way, Mordecai will be impaled on the stake and his body left dangling there in disgrace and humiliation. Mordecai's hanging corpse would be a monument to Haman's power and a balm for his wounded pride.

An Unexpected Development

Sometimes a king's life is so stressful it causes insomnia. Ahasuerus can't sleep. Josephus, in his retelling of the Esther story, comments that God took the king's sleep. Rabbinic legends report that God sends down the angel Michael, leader of the angelic hosts, to keep the king awake. The angel Gabriel descends as well, and tosses the king out of bed hundreds of times, whispering, "O thou ingrate, reward him who deserves to be rewarded." According to the legends, being awake is troubling to the king. Ahasuerus believes his wakefulness is due to being poisoned at dinner. He decides to execute the cooks, but they convince him no wrong was done, since Esther and Haman shared the meal and are not sick or dying.

The rabbis suggest Ahasuerus is tossing and turning because he suspects Haman and Esther may have concocted a plan against him. Perhaps they want him out of the way so they can be together. He

"That night the king could not sleep; so he ordered the book of the chronicles, the record of his reign, to be brought in and read to him. It was found recorded there that Mordecai had exposed [Bagathan and Thares], two of the king's officers who guarded the doorway, who had conspired to assassinate King [Ahasuerus]. 'What honor and recognition has Mordecai received for this?' the king asked. 'Nothing has been done for him,' his attendants answered" (Esther 6:1–3).

rules the idea out, though, believing his friends at court would have warned him about it.

Persian kings, according to Herodotus, considered it a moral duty to reward friends, or subjects who acted favorably. At the battle of Salamis, two Persian officers named Theomestor and Phylacus distinguished themselves in battle, capturing Greek ships. Herodotus writes "Theomestor in reward for this service was invested by the Persians with the lordship of Samos, and Phylacus was enrolled in the catalogue of the King's Benefactors and presented with a large estate."

Ahasuerus begins to worry he may not have adequately compensated his friends for services rendered. He wonders, according to Ginzberg, "[if it was] possible that by leaving valuable services unrewarded, he had forfeited the friendly feelings toward him? He therefore commanded, on this sleepless night, the chronicles of the kings of Persia be read to him. He would compare his own acts with what his predecessors had done, and try to find out whether he might count upon friends."

Josephus's account implies that rather than wasting time lying awake, Ahasuerus decides to do something advantageous to the kingdom, so he commands the scribes to bring in the chronicles of past kings and his own record. "While this was being read to him, the passage occurred in which Mordecai reported Bagathan and Teresh, two of the royal eunuchs who guarded the entrance, for seeking to lay hands on King Ahasuerus. The king asked, 'What was done to reward and honor Mordecai for this?' The king's attendants replied, 'Nothing was done for him'" (Esther 6:1–3).

Ahasuerus demands to know who of his advisors might be in the court. It is by now early morning, and the king needs advice. A tremendous omission of the ruler's moral duty has occurred. Mordecai has earned recognition and reward, but what is the best way to repay him for his past services?

JUST A COINCIDENCE?

Adele Berlin calls the entire book of Esther a comedy, and singles out this particular chapter as the "funniest anywhere in the Bible. The plot is constructed on coincidence, misunderstanding, reversal."

If Albert Einstein was correct in stating, "Coincidence is God's way of remaining anonymous," then God remains present throughout the activities of Esther 6. Einstein is not alone in this belief. Biblical scholars and others frequently cite coincidence as the evidence for God's presence. The 1844 poem "The Present Crisis" by James Russell Lowell states, "behind the dim unknown/standeth God within the shadow, keeping watch above his own." But God does more than just keep watch—sometimes, God uses "coincidence" to intervene on behalf of his own.

Coincidentally, the moment Ahasuerus asks whether any advisors have arrived at the palace, Haman is approaching on a mission of his own. Standing in the inner court, waiting for someone to notice him, he hopes to gain an early audience with the king. It has been a long night for Haman, too. His murderous thoughts made it impossible for him to sleep. As the Psalmist writes:

> An oracle is within my heart
>   concerning the sinfulness of the wicked:
>   There is no fear of God
>   before his eyes.
> For in his own eyes he flatters himself
>   too much to detect or hate his sin.
> The words of his mouth are wicked and deceitful;
>   he has ceased to be wise and to do good.
> Even on his bed he plots evil;
>   he commits himself to a sinful course
>   and does not reject what is wrong. (Psalm 36:1–4)

The king's servants, ever watchful for potential intruders, spot Haman lurking in the courtyard. "Haman is here," they tell Ahasuerus. "Send him in!" shouts the king in eager anticipation of garnering the advice he needs to properly and belatedly honor Mordecai. The two men, each driven by their own particular agendas, stand eye to eye. These agendas are mirror opposites: Haman wishes to disgrace and destroy Mordecai, while Ahasuerus wants to honor him. But kings get to speak first.

"What should be done for the man whom the king wishes to reward?" (Esther 6:6). The question catches Haman totally by surprise. For a moment his thoughts about dispatching Mordecai fade, and focus instead on his favorite subject: himself. "Whom would the king more probably wish to reward than me?" he thinks (Esther 6:6).

Josephus's version leaves more reason for Haman to misunderstand. Ahasuerus says, "Because I know that you are my only fast friend, I desire you to give me advice how I may honor one that I greatly love, and that after a manner suitable to my magnificence." In Haman's own mind, Haman is the one beloved of the king. Who else could be?

DREAMS OF A ROYAL LIFE

Greek literature of the fifth century, as well as other biblical sources, list the kinds of gifts given as tokens of honor. Horses with golden bridles, gold jewelry, gold daggers, and Persian robes are high priorities. Purple clothing, golden drinking cups, golden beds, fine linen turbans, necklaces, and seating adjacent to the king contribute to the possibilities. But Haman's ideas reflect his true desires.

Berlin quotes Pirke de-Rabbi Eliezer, a ninth century C.E. text that is part of the Midrash: "Haman said in his heart: He does not desire to exalt any other man except me. I will speak words so that I shall be king just as he is. He said to him: Let them bring the apparel which the king wore on the day of the coronation, and [let them bring] the horse upon which the king rode on the coronation day, and the crown which was put upon the head of the king on the day of coronation." Haman's chosen format for being honored is symbolic and significant.

In Haman's view, the man honored by the king should wear the king's own robe, the garment viewed as containing the very essence of the king's power. One honored by a king should also ride the king's own horse, not just any steed, and parade about the citadel to the intoning of long proclamations to his honor. The horse must be decked out in full regalia.

The image of riding the king's mount in a public place is symbolic of kingship itself. In 1 Kings 1:32–49, David orders Solomon to be placed on the king's mule, taken to the place of anointing, made king, and then returned to sit on the throne. Haman wants Susa to see him in his glory. If the procession should happen to pass the king's gate while Mordecai is there, all the better. That will show Haman's doomed enemy who is truly worthy of respect.

Haman already has the signet ring. People of the court, except Mordecai, bow and grovel. The only thing missing from his wish list is Queen Esther, and the rabbis have already hinted she may be on his mind. Many scholars agree: Haman just can't wait to be king.

Surprise!

After hearing Haman's suggestions, Ahasuerus is quick to agree to them. He commands Haman: "Hurry! Take the robe and horse as you have proposed, and do this for the Jew Mordecai, who is sitting at the royal gate. Do not omit anything you proposed" (Esther 6:10).

Haman has no choice but to comply with the king's command. Even grand viziers do not argue with kings. Haman must now honor his greatest enemy, the man he wished to kill. Haman must prepare the clothing and saddle; he must lead the horse and proclaim through the streets Mordecai's special honor by the king. It is a perfect reversal, a twist of fate. Haman is shocked speechless.

An Unexpected Development

Persian carvings like this one from Persepolis show ornately decorated horses such as the one Haman requests, complete with headdresses and plumage that might be described as being crown-like.

The Midrash discusses how Ahasuerus was forewarned by angels in a dream about Haman's true desires. The angel Michael whispers in his ear how Haman wants to kill him and become king. Ahasuerus dreams Haman approaches him with evil intent, and then wakes to find Haman standing at his bedside. Haman's wish list shows he desires not only the trappings of kingship, but the office as well. So, according to the rabbinical account, Ahasuerus "sets him up" for the fall.

The Midrash also recounts Haman's evasive attitude when Ahasuerus tells him to honor Mordecai; he pretends not to know who or where Mordecai is. He argues with the king about proper gifts to give Mordecai, recommending that Mordecai be made ruler over a city or district.

How much better that would be than forcing Haman to lead Mordecai on horseback throughout the citadel, announcing Mordecai's position of honor with the king.

Other Midrash suggests Haman first needed to wash Mordecai, who was filthy after having sat mourning in ashes. Once Mordecai was cleaned up and his steed prepared, Haman had to kneel down so Mordecai could step on his neck to mount the horse.

Ginzberg relates another legend, in which Haman's daughter is standing on a rooftop as her father comes by, leading Mordecai on the king's horse. Haman's face is understandably downcast, and Haman's daughter assumes that the man wearing finery on the horse is her father. She flings a chamber pot at the man leading the horse, thinking it to be Mordecai. The contents splash over her father. When she recognizes what she's done, she falls from the roof and dies.

Haman is shamed, mortified—in mourning (and covered in excrement, according to the rabbis). Mordecai slips off the horse, dons his street clothes, and returns to his post at the gate. What he must have been thinking during his ride is not stated. The rabbis comment that he went back to fasting and praying, donning his sackcloth, ever the pious Jew. Everything will be the same for him . . . he is safe . . . for now. Haman, head covered, slinks home. Nothing will be the same for him—and little does he know just how different his life will be. His hours, in fact, are numbered.

Home in Defeat

When he reports to his wife, friends, and advisors what has happened, Zeresh informs him things are only going to get worse; she bluntly predicts Haman has no chance of prevailing against Mordecai if he is a Jew. It is strange they failed to point out that fact earlier, when they encouraged him to build the instrument of death and step up the slaughter by a few months.

Scholars note this change of heart as another veiled reference to God in the story. Bechtel calls this reaction by Haman's former supporters a "foreigner's confession" of faith. "Although [they] never actually confess their faith in the God of the Jews, they seem to have a kind of superstitious sense of the Jews' superiority," Bechtel writes. "The tide . . . has turned against Haman, and they seem only too anxious to abandon ship." Haman's friends are pulling away, leaving him to stand alone against opposing forces—including Yahweh.

Haman's gibbet will not serve the purpose he intended, because his plan for the early destruction of Mordecai has been squelched—the king will never agree to the execution of someone he has just honored. In addition, Ahasuerus has acknowledged Mordecai is Jewish. How will the king react when he learns Haman has issued an edict in the king's name to destroy Mordecai and every other Jew?

That edict against the Jews still stands, however. Mordecai has dodged disaster for the moment, but unless Esther can bring her plan to fruition, all may still be lost. Now, with Haman's gibbet of death visible out the window, there is a knock at the door. The eunuchs have come to escort Haman to dinner with the king and queen.

Justice and an Unstoppable Edict

In the book of Esther, the last time a group of eunuchs guided someone to a banquet, that someone was Queen Vashti. If Haman remembered what happened there, he might have been reluctant to accept Queen Esther's second dinner invitation. But he goes, apparently hopeful that the party will cheer him up. With his wife's prediction of doom in his ears, with the memory of leading Mordecai through the streets like royalty, Haman imbibes his after-dinner wine. Ahasuerus, relaxed with his drinking, reclining on his couch, looks at his Queen and follows up on his question from the preceding night. "Whatever you ask, Queen Esther, shall be granted you. Whatever request you make shall be honored, even for half the kingdom" (Esther 7:2).

The Hebrew Alpha Text, influenced along the way with Greek elements, relates that Esther is nervous, "because the enemy was right in front of her, but God gave her the courage for the

Justice and an Unstoppable Edict 83

The 17th century Dutch master Rembrandt painted this scene of Esther, Ahasuerus, and Haman at the queen's banquet.

challenge." The Masoretic text does not involve God, however; in this account the courage to speak is Queen Esther's alone. Though she might have started from the beginning, retelling all the events, and perhaps confusing Ahasuerus, she begins instead with an emotional message that caters to the king's protective nature. "If I have found favor with you, O king, and if it pleases your majesty, I ask that my life be spared, and I beg that you spare the lives of my people. For my people have been delivered to destruction, slaughter, and extinction" (Esther 7:3–4).

Esther has the king's attention. Ahasuerus now knows two things he did not know: his wife is a Jew, and her life is in danger because of Haman's edict. There may be a flash of understanding that by empowering Haman to write and seal the edict, Ahasuerus himself is responsible for the threat to Esther's life. Esther continues, "If we were to be sold into slavery I would remain silent, but as it is, the enemy will be unable to compensate for the harm done to the king" (Esther 7:4).

This passage plays on the similarities between the Hebrew words "to destroy" and "to enslave." Apparently, somehow Esther has learned how the king was tricked into agreeing to the destructive decree by clever words that carry a double meaning. She knows about Haman's bribe; she understands that the king may have believed he was agreeing to enslave some troublemakers.

Adele Berlin goes a step further in discussing what is meant by enslavement. "On one level, in ancient Near Eastern terminology being someone's 'slave' can simply mean recognizing the superior authority of that person," she writes. "From a Jewish perspective, enslavement could mean to be under the sovereignty of a foreign ruler, which the Jews were to the Persian king. [The] Jews were satisfied with the status quo and would gladly reaffirm their

Ancient Banquets

Banquets are a central motif in the book of Esther; the book begins and ends with banquets, and many important events, good and evil, occur at a banquet. One word used for banquet or feast is *mishteh*, literally "drinking."

In ancient times, the banquet was a great social event. Guests were washed and anointed with fragrant oils, and, in Persia, then reclined on couches to be served their meal. There were rich dishes, varieties of wine, the largest portions reserved for the guest of honor.

Typically, entertainment followed the meal, such as music, storytelling, and dancing.

loyalty to the Persian king." But Esther implies a darker, more sinister motive, Berlin notes: "To sell the Jews into slavery implies that they are being wrested away from the sovereignty of the king and given over to another power. This is a treasonous offense. If this is what Haman had proposed, then he is a traitor to the king."

Ahasuerus could easily interpret Haman's action as an attempt to usurp kingly power. "Who and where . . . is the man who has dared to do this?" roars the king in Esther 7:5, defending the royal honor. "The enemy oppressing us is this wicked Haman," responds the Queen (Esther 7:6). Her plan has played out without a hitch.

HAMAN'S LAST STAND

According to Louis Ginzberg's retelling of the legend, Esther next sums up all of Haman's evil acts:

> This is the adversary and the enemy, he who desired to murder thee in thy sleeping-chamber during the night just passed; he who this very day desired to array himself in the royal apparel, ride upon thy horse, and wear the golden crown upon his head, to rise up against thee and deprive thee of thy sovereignty. But God set his undertaking at naught, and the honors he sought for himself, fell to the share of my [cousin] Mordecai who this oppressor and enemy thought to hang.

Haman is seized with dread, frozen with fear. The king, perhaps to gather his thoughts, perhaps because he does not know what else to do, stomps out in a rage, leaving Haman alone with the Queen. Haman's only chance is to beg the Queen to intercede for him, or he is doomed. He falls on her feet as she lays on her couch—a bad idea. Ahasuerus bursts back into the room. If the king had not been able to decide what to do with Haman yet, he knows now. According to Josephus, the king says to Haman, "O you wretch . . . you vilest of mankind, do you aim to rape my wife?" Haman's face was "covered over," meaning red with embarrassment, or drained of its color, pale with fear.

This incident gives the king some cover as he decides what to do with his disloyal grand vizier. If Ahasuerus punished Haman only on the basis of the decree against the Jews, the king would betray his own stupidity at having been duped. After all, the king's signet ring had sealed the Jews' fate. But a sexual assault on the queen would be reason enough to dispose of Haman.

As Ahasuerus ponders Haman's fate, a court eunuch named Harbonah informs the king, "At the house of Haman stands a gibbet fifty cubits high. Haman prepared it for Mordecai who gave the report that benefited the king" (Esther 7:9). Ahasuerus, with all the assurance of the true monarch, orders, "'Hang him on it.' So they hanged Haman on the gibbet which he had made ready for Mordecai, and the anger of the king abated" (Esther 7:9, 10). Haman has been hoist with his own petard, a victim of circumstances brought on by himself. Ironically, he is executed on the stake he'd intended for Mordecai—a perfect reversal.

The Evolution of Esther

Following Haman's demise, Ahasuerus begins to right the wrongs done to Esther and Mordecai. The king gives all of Haman's wealth and property to Esther. If Esther was rich simply by becoming queen, then words cannot describe the value of her personal holdings at receipt of this "inheritance" from Haman.

It was not unusual for an estate to be absorbed into the king's possessions. Josephus, citing the words of Cyrus of

Justice and an Unstoppable Edict 87

This illustration from a 12th century French Bible shows Esther kneeling before the king (top left), and the hanging of Haman (bottom left). It seems fitting that Haman, being a perpetrator of half truths, is ultimately punished for something he did not intend to do: assaulting the queen.

Persia, writes, "The priests shall also offer these sacrifices according to the laws of Moses in Jerusalem; and when they offer them, they shall pray to God for the preservation of the king and his family, that the kingdom of Persia may continue. But my will is, that those who disobey these injunctions, and make them void, shall be hung upon a cross, and their substance brought into the king's treasury."

THE IMPACT OF WEALTH

The concept of wealth is central to three characters in the story of Esther: Ahasuerus, Haman, and Esther herself. But its effect on each person differs.

Ahasuerus, as ruler of the Persian Empire, inherited his wealth without effort, and added to it with military conquests of neighboring nations, enabling his kingdom to stretch from India to Ethiopia. His wealth provided him a lavish lifestyle, and enabled the king to built great shrines and monuments to himself. However, using his wealth to glorify himself does not make Ahasuerus an effective king; according to the tale, he cannot make even the simplest decisions without help. Ahasuerus only begins to look and act like a king when a strong queenly presence, Esther, arrives on the scene.

Haman's wealth was legendary among the rabbis. According to them, he had managed to acquire the treasuries of the Judean kings and of the temple; he was so rich his bribe to Ahasuerus had equaled two-thirds of the wealth of the Persian Empire, according to scholarly interpretation. But Haman's wealth served no useful purpose except to advance his personal agenda. Money was useful in enabling him to get what he wanted, no matter who was destroyed in the process. In the end, however, Haman's money could not save him, and he died on the stake that he had paid workmen to erect for Mordecai.

As queen, Esther already shared in the tremendous wealth of the Persian Empire. With the death of Haman, she received her own nest egg, courtesy of the king. Having inherited Haman's estate, Esther's wealth was extraordinary. She made Mordecai the estate manager, but retained possession and control.

The story might have ended here had Esther's personality been anything like that of Ahasuerus or Haman. She might have lived out her life in extravagance and leisure and forgotten all about the plight of her people. But Esther remains true to the mission to save the Jews, so she uses her power and influence for the benefit of others.

THE NEW ORDER

After the death of Haman, the king invites Mordecai to the palace. Knowing he is Esther's kinsman, the king gives Mordecai the signet ring that has been removed from Haman's finger. Mordecai becomes the new grand vizier in place of his enemy.

The reversal seems complete—a new beginning beckons, except for one small fact. The edict against the Jews is still in force. Esther's work isn't over yet. She falls at the king's feet, begging him to stop Haman's evil plan to annihilate the Jews. When the king extends his scepter to her, indicating a willingness to listen, she stands, and restates her request:

> "If it pleases your majesty and seems proper to you, and if I have found favor with you and you love me, let a document be issued to revoke the letters which that schemer Haman, son of Hammedatha, the Agagite, wrote for the destruction for the Jews in all the royal provinces. For how can I witness the evil that is to befall my people, and how can I behold the destruction of my race?" (Esther 8:5, 6).

By naming Haman, Esther identifies the evil edict as Haman's doing; anything Ahasuerus might have had to do with the decree (i.e., giving Haman his ring and the freedom to write it) is not an issue. Michael Fox comments that the length of the preamble to her petition indicates she is not sure how the king will react; there is a feeling, notes Fox, that Esther is no longer a future victim of the pogrom, but she is pleading for her people's salvation.

The tone of Ahasuerus's answer suggests that he wants nothing more to do with the matter. He reminds Esther he has given Haman's estate to her and has had Haman executed. Then he tells Esther and Mordecai (the *you* in Hebrew is plural): "You in turn may write in the king's name what you see fit concerning the Jews and seal the letter with the royal signet ring. For whatever is written in the name of the king and sealed with the royal signet ring cannot be revoked" (Esther 8:8).

According to the king, therefore, Persian laws are irrevocable. The only thing that can stop the unstoppable edict is a new edict of equal power and authority. The king has given Esther and Mordecai license to create it. Nine months remain until the 13th of Adar. There is no time to lose.

From Battle Day to Holiday

In the closing chapters of the book (Chapters 8–10), Esther and Mordecai function as a team, writing and authenticating new edicts to cancel Haman's mission. They rise to positions of respect and power—for peace and prosperity, and together insure the remembrance of the events in the celebration of Purim.

The royal scribes are summoned; when they arrive, Mordecai dictates a letter, addressed to "the Jews and to the satraps, governors, and officials of the hundred and twenty-seven provinces from India to Ethiopia: to each province in its own script and to each people in its own language, and the Jews in their own script and language. These letters, which he wrote in the name of King Ahasuerus and sealed with the royal signet ring, he sent by mounted couriers riding thoroughbred royal steeds" (Esther 9–10).

Within three months, the time it takes for the riders to reach the outer boundary of the regime, all inhabitants of the kingdom receive a copy of Mordecai's letter. In the Masoretic account, the message is described as follows:

> The king's edict granted the Jews in every city the right to assemble and protect themselves; to destroy, kill and annihilate any armed force of any nationality or province that might attack them and their women and children; and to plunder the property of their enemies. The day appointed for the Jews to do this in all the provinces of King [Ahasuerus] was the thirteenth day of the twelfth month, the month of Adar. A copy of the text of the edict was to be issued as law in every province and made known to the people of every nationality so that the Jews would be ready on that day to avenge themselves on their enemies. (Esther 8:11–13)

Scholars note the almost point by point match of Mordecai's and Haman's letters. For the Jewish recipients, the good news is this letter has the seal of the signet upon it—it is an irrevocable law.

Some readers are uncomfortable with the level of violence advocated in the book of Esther. Michael Fox holds the position that the Jews receive permission to kill everyone necessary in order to defend themselves, but that they will not initiate the violence. Carey Moore comments that

---

Most historians agree that the unstoppable edict is merely a dramatic plot device. It is critical to the tension in the story of Esther, but it would be difficult for a kingdom to function if royal edicts could not be revoked as circumstances dictated.

The Importance of Mordecai

Mordecai's role in the Esther story is critical. Some scholars go so far as to suggest that Mordecai is more of a hero than Esther. His job at the palace gate, his saving of the king from would-be assassins, his vigilance regarding Esther's safety and well-being, and his knowledge of the intricacies of palace life all support the overturning of Haman's edict. Mordecai's connections at the palace allow him to give Esther the information she needs to persuade the king. Without Mordecai's creative wailing outside the palace gate, Esther might never have known what was going on until it was too late. Purim was once referred to as "the Day of Mordecai."

by giving Jews permission to fight, some attacks on Jewish communities may be deterred.

The rules set forth in this letter follow the ancient Israelite rules of warfare. When nations outside the Promised Land waged war against the people of Israel, men were slain, but women, children, cattle, and property were taken as spoil. Against Canaanites, though, all people and goods were "devoted to God" and had to be destroyed.

Mordecai's Greek Decree

The Septuagint version of the story places Addition E at this point; this Addition contains the supposed text of the letter of Mordecai. It presents a different tone than the letter described in Esther 8:11, however. The Septuagint letter is written in the king's voice, confessing how he was led astray by the wicked Haman, a Macedonian (foreigner), not an Agagite as portrayed by the Masoretic text. The letter warns against Persians attacking the Jews in any way; in fact, it encourages Persians to help the Jews in their fight against their enemies. The king speaks favorably about God: how Haman arrogantly believed he could escape God's judgement; how the Jews are law-abiding, children of the Living God. The Addition advocates the letter of Haman be ignored, informing the recipients of Haman's execution. The Jews are empowered to defend themselves, and Persians are warned that God will intervene to protect His people. Persians are encouraged to celebrate Purim along with the Jews; those who do not celebrate the holiday will "be ruthlessly destroyed with fire and sword" (Addition E:24).

It is interesting that Purim is mentioned, since according to the Masoretic account Purim occurs as a spontaneous celebration after battles on the 13th of Adar. Mordecai, allegedly writing this edict in the name of Ahasuerus, makes the king seem like quite a zealot. Carol Bechtel comments, "Even if we grant that it is Mordecai who is ghostwriting the edict, this version of the king sounds like he is ready to convert."

The people of the empire receive the message, and the Jews prepare to defend themselves. Mordecai is elevated to royal status, clothed in purple and white, with a gold turban and crimson cloak—he attains the status Haman dreamed of but never achieved. There is a tremendous outcry of joy in the citadel of Susa, followed by merriment and exaltation, feasts and banquets. As recorded in Proverbs 11:10, "When the just prosper, the city rejoices; and when the wicked perish, there is jubilation."

Esther 8:16 says that many non-believers in Persia convert to Judaism at this time. This may indicate that these converts feared God, or may simply mean that many Persians sympathized with the Jews and sided with them. The conversion to Judaism of large numbers of Persians is is not recorded in extra-biblical literature dating from this time period, however.

Mordecai's letter infers that Jewish military success will be inevitable. Adele Berlin believes this was meant as another comic motif of the story. "The unlikelihood of non-Jews fearing the military strength of the Jews is just one more of many implausibilities in the book," she writes. "All of this should be understood in the spirit of the carnivalesque, where reality is turned on its head. Only in a carnivalesque fiction could a small Jewish minority be given such power."

BATTLE DAYS!

When the 13th of Adar arrives, the united Jews meet the forces opposing them, and no one can overcome them. The leaders of local governments support the Jews out of

This bas-relief from the palace of Darius I at Persepolis depicts spear-carrying Persian soldiers. The edict of Haman and counter-edict of Esther and Mordecai creates the prospect of civil warfare within the Persian Empire.

fear of Mordecai. Esther's relative has risen to such high importance in Ahasuerus's court that the provincial governors fear his power.

The reports from the battlefields pour in. The Jews have struck down their enemies at every turn. In Susa, five hundred are killed, among them the ten sons of Haman. There is no plundering of goods, however—for the Jews, the focus of this battle is self-defense, not acquisition of wealth or property. At the end of the first day of battle, the king summons Esther. He comments on the battle, and

Detail from an ancient Hebrew manuscript of Esther, probably Persian in origin, showing the hanging of Haman's sons.

reminds Esther that he will do anything she asks. Some commentators suggest this passage is another indirect reference to God, indicating that Ahasuerus is so afraid of God that he will do whatever Esther tells him.

Esther's response, unlike her past conversations with the king, does not begin with a long, formal speech. This seems to be evidence of a new, more relaxed and informal relationship between the king and queen. She asks "that the Jews in Susa be permitted again tomorrow to act according to today's decree, and let the ten sons of Haman be hanged on gibbets." (Esther 9:13). The king duly gives the order, and another three hundred are killed on the 14th of Adar. The bodies of the ten sons of Haman are hanged for all to see.

The order for this second day of fighting is for Susa only; fighting in the rest of the Persian provinces occurs only on the 13th of Adar. The Bible says that overall, the Jews kill 75,000 enemies in self defense.

Adele Berlin believes that the level of violence described in Esther should not be taken seriously:

> The number of the slain enemies . . . has troubled the many commentators who take this chapter as serious revenge. But this number should be understood as being just as exaggerated as the other numbers in the story . . . this overkill is not real killing. There is no way that the relatively small Jewish communities in Persia could kill so many people. We are in that realm of carnivalesque fantasy. To be sure, inflated body counts are tradition in Assyrian annals, where they are not carnivalesque. The purpose of the large number of dead is to give more glory to the conquering king and his god. The same purpose may be implied in Esther as well: it is to the credit of the Jews (and their unmentioned God) that they were so successful."

The fighting ends after the 14th of Adar. The Susa Jews rest, rejoice, and feast on the 15th. The other provinces have already done the same on the 14th. This led to a Jewish custom that people living in fortified cities that existed in Esther's time (ie., Jerusalem) celebrate Purim on the 15th, while those living in other communities celebrate Purim on the 14th.

A Festival Is Established

Mordecai soon sends another message, in which he tells the Jews of Persia to:

> celebrate annually the fourteenth and fifteenth days of the month of Adar as the time when the Jews got relief from their enemies, and as the month when their sorrow was turned into joy and their mourning into a day of celebration. He wrote them to observe the days as days of feasting and joy and giving presents of food to one another and gifts to the poor.
> So the Jews agreed to continue the celebration they had begun, doing what Mordecai had written to them (Esther 9:21–23).

Many textual critics believe the etiology, or explanation, for the origins of Purim given in Esther 9:18–32 was not part of the original story. Details in this summary do not match other parts of the story: the king is given credit for exposing Haman and his plot against the Jews, for example, and for having Haman and his sons impaled on gibbets because of their involvement in the plot.

Michael Fox argues that Mordecai, in his role as grand vizier, is purposely giving Ahasuerus the credit for being the catalyst—he is, after all, the king. "He encourages the king to adopt attitudes beneficial to the Jews by flattering him for having these attitudes already," writes Fox. "By depicting the Jews as more passive than in the earlier narrative, the summary reflects the way Jews must operate in the foreign court: they must make the ruler do their will by making him think it is his own."

Fox goes on to examine the word "Purim," calling into question the relation between it and the word *pur*. Fox notes that if Haman had cast a lot (singular) it would not explain why the festival was named Purim (lots, plural). He suggests "the holiday and its name existed before the book of Esther was composed and that the author is making an effort to connect the two" to create an explanation for the celebration. In fact, Greek references in the second Book of Maccabees—a text that was included in the Septuagint and is considered canonical by Roman Catholics and Eastern Orthodox Christians, but not by Jews and Protestants—call the holiday "the day of Mordecai" (II Maccabees 15:36). Other Greek texts refer to it as *phrourai* or *phourdaia*. The particular name, it seems, is less important than the underlying emotion of salvation and peace for the future.

A traditional gragger, or noisemaker, used during the celebration of Purim. Whenever the name of Haman is spoken during the reading of the Esther megillah, the audience in the synagogue spins graggers, boos, shouts catcalls, and stamps feet to drown out his evil name.

Copy of the story of Esther in Hebrew, opened to the list of Haman's sons. Public readings of Esther's story are an important part of the Purim celebration. The megillah is read twice: once on the eve of Purim, and again on the day. A tradition recommends that those listening to the reading follow along in a copy of Esther, so as not to miss a single word of the story.

Queen Esther has the last word, sending a letter to the provinces and cities that confirms the requirement to follow Mordecai's guidelines for the festival. Purim has been established as a holiday for Jews in both present and future generations.

The biblical account ends with Ahasuerus back in control of his empire. It notes that the king's exploits, and those of his second-in-command, Mordecai, are recorded in the royal annals.

THE GREEK ANTICLIMAX

The Septuagint concludes the book of Esther with Addition F, an interpretation of Mordecai's dream that opened the Greek account. The symbolisms of the dream are explained, and God is given glory for saving his people by working great signs and wonders. The tiny stream that grew into a river was Esther, the battling dragons were Haman and Mordecai, and the nations were the people who endeavored to destroy the Jews—all in vain, for the Jews, thanks to God's intervention, prevailed against them. The Addition mentions two lots, one drawn for the Jews, and one for the nations, each being fulfilled in its own way; with this, the author of the Addition attempts to insert a final link between story and festival.

The Greek text ends with a postscript that says, "In the fourth year of the reign of Ptolemy and Cleopatra, Dositheus, who said he was a priest and Levite, and his son Ptolemy brought the present letter of Purim, saying that it was genuine and that Lysimachus, son of Ptolemy, of the community of Jerusalem, had translated it." This postscript probably dates to about 78 or 77 B.C.E. Carol Bechtel explains its presence by noting, "[The] author thought it was important to attest in whatever way he could to the authenticity of 'Purim.' His passion attests to the presence of a living community of faith that valued the book he had received."

Conclusion

While most scholars today agree that Esther was written as an explanation for the origins of Purim, it is also a strongly nationalistic story of how Jews managed to survive as a people against powerful odds in a foreign land.

Drinking During Purim

A festival meal and the consumption of wine are important parts of the Purim celebration. In fact, drinking on Purim is *mitzvah* (law), not just a casual suggestion. The Talmud says that Jews must drink on Purim until they can no longer distinguish between the phrases *arur Haman* ("Cursed is Haman") and *baruch Mordechai* ("Blessed is Mordecai"). In this, Purim is reminiscent of the great drinking parties given by Ahasuerus.

Today, drinking too much wine during Purim is a potential problem for many Jewish communities. Over the years rabbis have pointed out that people must not drink so much that others are hurt or endangered, or that Jewish laws are broken. Those who need to drive or to take care of others should not drink, for example.

Inebriated or sober, on Purim Jews are reminded that Yahweh is with them. They are encouraged to contemplate God, put away anguish and fear, and work to build relationships with others.

Esther is unique among Bible books in that—certainly in the version accepted as canonical by Jews and Protestant Christians—the book never mentions God's name or presence directly. (Though later Additions seek to make the story more God-centered, scholars have noted they stand out in form and content from the main core of the story.) The Masoretic text offers hints at God's activity in the story, but in general irony and coincidence are the only means by which God's presence can be identified. Perhaps the message of Esther is that even though God seems absent, God is always present, working to ensure the safety and well being of His people.

The book also provides an example of how people who have been blessed with wealth and power ought to behave. Esther goes from being a lowly Jewish maiden to becoming the wealthy and powerful queen of Persia. But despite her tremendous wealth, Esther is not blind to the needs of others. The story of Esther illustrates that individuals must respond when they learn about wrongdoing or threats to innocents, no matter what the prospective consequences to themselves. As Mordecai tells Esther (4:14):

> For if you remain silent at this time, relief and deliverance . . . will arise from another place. . . . And who knows but that you have come to royal position for such a time as this?

Notes

CHAPTER ONE: THE SCROLL

p. 12: "We can no longer assume…" Carol M. Bechtel, *Esther: Interpretation* (Louisville, Ky.: John Knox Press, 2002), p. 17.

p. 16: "I am so hostile…" Martin Luther, quoted in Floyd V. Filson, *Which Books Belong in the Bible* (Philadelphia: The Westminster Press, 1957), p. 10.

p. 17: "Like most of the Bible…" Michael V. Fox, *Character and Ideology in the Book of Esther* (Grand Rapids: Eerdmans Publishing Co., 2001), p. 254.

p. 17: "The AT is preserved in…" Fox, *Character and Ideology in the Book of Esther*, p. 255.

p. 18: "Indeed, the author of Esther…" Adele Berlin, *The JPS Bible Commentary: Esther* (Philadelphia: The Jewish Publication Society, 2001), p. xlii

p. 20: "Perhaps the Essenes resented the…" Ginsberg and Bardtke, quoted in Carey A. Moore, *Esther* (New York: Doubleday, 1971), p. xxii.

p. 22: "This story seems to have…" Berlin, *The JPS Bible Commentary: Esther*, p. xv.

p. 23: "Some post-exilic Jews…" Sandra Beth Berg, *The Book of Esther: Motifs, Themes, and Structure* (Cedar Falls: The Society of Biblical Literature, 1979), p. 141.

p. 25: "the romance's favorite themes and…" Fox, *Character and Ideology in the Book of Esther*, p. 145.

p. 26: "Although I doubt the historicity…" Fox, *Character and Ideology in the Book of Esther*, p. 11.

CHAPTER TWO: IN SEARCH OF A QUEEN

p. 29: "The central theme of the…" Bernhard W. Anderson, *Understanding the Old Testament* (Englewood Cliffs: Prentice-Hall, Inc., 1975), pp. 577, 578.

p. 31: "Chapter 1 sets the tone of…" Berlin, *The JPS Bible Commentary: Esther*, p. 3.

p. 32: "In Greek sources, Xerxes is…" Berlin, *The JPS Bible Commentary: Esther*, p. 5.

p. 34: "inscriptions on tablets deposited in…" Berlin, *The JPS Bible Commentary: Esther*, p. 7.

p. 35: "The splendor…is the gauge…" Louis Ginzberg, *The Legends of the Jews*, vol. IV (Charleston: BiblioBazaar, 2007), p. 249.

p. 36: "the upper branches of the…" Ginzberg, *The Legends of the Jews*, p. 253.

p. 36: "If an important decision is…" Herodotus, *The Histories* (London: Penguin, 1972), page 97.

p. 37: "'Their God,' says Haman…" Ginzberg, *The Legends of the Jews*, p. 252.

p. 38: "Nice queens don't go to…" Berlin, *The JPS Bible Commentary: Esther*, p. 11.

p. 39: "the weak and unsteady despot…" Fox, *Character and Ideology in the Book of Esther*, p. 25.

p. 39: "In short," says commentator Carol…" Bechtel, *Esther: Interpretation*, p. 26.

p. 40: "Thereupon Ahasuerus issued a decree…" Ginzberg, *The Legends of the Jews*, p. 260.

p. 41: "if one pictures the Persian…" Fox, *Character and Ideology in the Book of Esther*, p. 33.

p. 42: "There are no parting gifts…" Bechtel, *Esther: Interpretation*, p. 31.

CHAPTER THREE: HAMAN'S REVENGE

p. 48: "Before such [a] one…" Ginzberg, *The Legends of the Jews*, p. 270.

p. 49: "Mordecai refuses to bow because…" Fox, *Character and Ideology in the Book of Esther*, p. 44.

p. 52: "The Jews were not the…" Fox, *Character and Ideology in the Book of Esther*, p. 48.

p. 52: "In this way they waste…" Ginzberg, *The Legends of the Jews*, p. 277.

p. 52: "In Ezra 4:12–16 it is claimed…" Berlin, *The JPS Bible Commentary: Esther*, p. 40.

p. 53: "While it is obvious that…" Bechtel, *Esther: Interpretation*, p. 43.

p. 54: "Haman's edict presumes that a…" Fox, *Character and Ideology in the Book of Esther*, p. 55.

CHAPTER FOUR: A TIME TO MOURN

p. 59: "a great spasm of grief." Bechtel, *Esther: Interpretation*, p. 45.

p. 59: "God is most present and…" Berlin, *The JPS Bible Commentary: Esther*, p. 44.

p. 60: "Now the king had made…" *The New Complete Works of Josephus*, trans. by William Whiston (Grand Rapids: Kregel Publications, 1999), p. 375.

p. 61: "Esther is not refusing the…" Berlin, *The JPS Bible Commentary: Esther*, p. 48.

p. 62: "The narrator believed in a…" Berg, *The Book of Esther: Motifs, Themes, and Structure*, p. 178.

p. 62: "This carefully crafted indeterminacy is…" Fox, *Character and Ideology in the Book of Esther*, p. 247.

p. 63: "One gets the impression that…" Bechtel, *Esther: Interpretation*, p. 93.

p. 64: "arrayed…in a silken garment…" Ginzberg, *The Legends of the Jews*, p. 290.

p. 64: "by reason of her long…" Ginzberg, *The Legends of the Jews*, p. 293.

CHAPTER FIVE: DINNER FOR THREE

p. 66: "royal business meeting…" Berlin, *The JPS Bible Commentary: Esther*, pp. 51, 52.

p. 66: "Dressing up to visit the…" Bechtel, *Esther: Interpretation*, p. 51.

p. 67: "Let the king come—and..." Bechtel, *Esther: Interpretation*, p. 52.

p. 68: "Postponing her real request another..." Moore, *Esther*, pp. 57, 58.

p. 69: "Haman felt secure in his..." Ginzberg, *The Legends of the Jews*, p. 294.

p. 69: "pointed to his knee, inscribed..." Ginzberg, *The Legends of the Jews*, p. 294.

p. 70: "After prowess in fighting, the..." Herodotus, *The Histories*, p. 98.

p. 71: "And all this is worthless..." Ginzberg, *The Legends of the Jews*, p. 294.

p. 71: "If the man thou tellest..." Ginzberg, *The Legends of the Jews*, p. 294.

p. 72: "Even Solomon's Temple is only..." Berlin, *The JPS Bible Commentary: Esther*, p. 55.

p. 72: "She fetched artificers in wood..." Ginzberg, *The Legends of the Jews*, p. 294.

CHAPTER SIX: AN UNEXPECTED DEVELOPMENT

p. 73: "O thou ingrate, reward him..." Ginzberg, *The Legends of the Jews*, p. 296.

p. 74: "Theomestor in reward for this..." Herodotus, *The Histories*, p. 551.

p. 75: "possible that by leaving valuable..." Ginzberg, *The Legends of the Jews*, p. 296.

p. 75: "funniest anywhere in the Bible..." Berlin, *The JPS Bible Commentary: Esther*, p. 56.

p. 75: "Coincidence is God's way of..." attributed to Albert Einstein, http://www.quoteworld.org/quotes/9886

p. 76: "behind the dim unknown, standeth..." James Russell Lowell, "Once to Every Man and Nation," *The Methodist Hymnal* (Nashville: The Methodist Publishing House, 1964), Hymn 242, vs. 4.

p. 77: "Because I know that you..." Whiston, *The New Complete Works of Josephus*, p. 378.

p. 77: "Haman said in his heart..." Berlin, *The JPS Bible*

	Commentary: Esther, p. 61.
p. 81:	Although [they] never actually confess..." Bechtel, *Esther: Interpretation*, p. 61.

CHAPTER SEVEN: JUSTICE AND AN UNSTOPPABLE EDICT

p. 82:	"because the enemy was right..." Moore, *Esther*, pp. 69, 70.
p. 84:	"On one level, in ancient..." Berlin, *The JPS Bible Commentary: Esther*, pp. 66, 67.
p. 85:	"To sell the Jews into..." Berlin, *The JPS Bible Commentary: Esther*, pp. 66, 67.
p. 85:	"This is the adversary and..." Ginzberg, *The Legends of the Jews*, p. 302.
p. 86:	"O you wretch..." Whiston, *The New Complete Works of Josephus*, p. 378.
p. 88:	"The priests shall also offer..." Whiston, *The New Complete Works of Josephus*, p. 360.

CHAPTER EIGHT: FROM BATTLE DAY TO HOLIDAY

p. 94:	"Even if we grant that..." Bechtel, *Esther: Interpretation*, p. 96.
p. 95:	"The unlikelihood of non-Jews..." Berlin, *The JPS Bible Commentary: Esther*, p. 81.
p. 97:	"The number of the slain..." Berlin, *The JPS Bible Commentary: Esther*, p. 87.
p. 98:	"He encourages the king to..." Fox, *Character and Ideology in the Book of Esther*, p. 120.
p. 99:	"the holiday and its name..." Fox, *Character and Ideology in the Book of Esther*, p. 121.
p. 101:	"In the fourth year of..." annotation in *The New American Bible* (Catholic Bible Publishers, 1987).
p. 101:	"[The] author thought it was..." Bechtel, *Esther: Interpretation*, pp. 97, 98.

Glossary

Apocrypha—a term coined by the fifth-century biblical scholar Saint Jerome that refers to the biblical books included as part of the Septuagint (the Greek version of the Old Testament) but not included in the Hebrew Bible (Masoretic text). These same books are referred to by Protestants as the pseudepigrapha.

Church Fathers—men whose written works served as the theological thought of the church in its first few centuries: Justin Martyr, Tertullian, Origen, Clement of Alexandria, etc.

cubit—a non-standard measurement, approximately the distance between the elbow and the tip of the middle finger.

Diaspora—refers to the community of "dispersed" Jews, living in foreign territory during and following a period of exile and restoration; the Jewish population living in Babylon after 586 B.C.E.

doctrine—a teaching or principle accepted by religious or philosophic group; dogma.

etiology—an explanation for a pre-existing situation.

faith—the unqualified acceptance of and dependence on the completed work of Christ to secure God's mercy.

Gentile—a non-Jew.

megillah—Hebrew word for "scroll"; often used to refer to the book of Esther.

Midrash—rabbinic thought and interpretation, sermonic in nature; imaginative commentary.

monotheism—the belief in one God.

obeisance—to do honor; to bow or prostrate oneself.

omnipotence—the unlimited power of God.

parable—a story in which a moral or spiritual truth is drawn by comparison.

Pentateuch—the first five books of the Hebrew scriptures.

providence—the belief that the events of life are not ruled by chance, but according to God's sovereign plan.

pseudepigrapha—a Greek term meaning "false inscription."

sackcloth—symbol of mourning or great despair; a garment worn instead of daily clothing, draped over oneself.

sedition—treason.

Targum—an Aramaic translation of the Hebrew Bible.

Torah—the five books of Moses, the written Law; Genesis, Exodus, Leviticus, Numbers, Deuteronomy; the Pentatuech.

Further Reading

BOOKS FOR YOUNG READERS

Blitz, Shmuel. *The Artscroll Children's Megillah* (Brooklyn, NY: Mesorah Publications, Ltd., 2003.

Fishman, Cathy Goldberg. *On Purim.* New York: Atheneum Books, 2000.

Gelman, Rita Golden. *Queen Esther Saves Her People.* New York: Scholastic Press, 1998.

Gerstein, Mordecai. *Queen Esther the Morning Star.* New York: Simon and Shuster, 2000.

Scherman, Nosson, and Meir Zlotowitz. *Artscroll Youth Megillah: Fully Illustrated with the Complete Text, Simplified Translation and Comments.* Brooklyn, NY: Mesorah Publications, 1988.

Silberman, Shoshana. *The Whole Megillah.* Rockville, Md: Kar-Ben Copies, Inc., 1990.

BOOKS FOR ADULTS

Apisdorf, Shimon. *The One Hour Purim Primer: Everything a Family Needs to Understand, Celebrate, and Enjoy Purim.* Baltimore: Leviathan Press, 1995.

Bechtel, Carol M. *Esther: Interpretation.* Louisville, Ky.: John Knox Press, 2002.

Berlin, Adele. *The JPS Bible Commentary: Esther* (Philadelphia: The Jewish Publication Society, 2001)

Cahn, Yoel T. *Links Beyond Time: The Book of Esther in Light of the Life of Yoseph.* Southfield, Mich.: Targum Publishers, 1995.

Fox, Michael V. *Character and Ideology in the Book of Esther*. Grand Rapids, Mich.: Eerdmans Publishing Co., 2001.

Ginzberg, Louis. *Legends of the Jews,* trans. by Henrietta Szold and Paul Radin. Philadelphia: the Jewish Publication Society, 2003.

Gold, Avie. *Purim: Its Observance and Significance—A Presentation based on Talmudic and Traditional Sources*. Brooklyn, NY: Mesorah Publications, Ltd., 1993.

Goodman, Philip. *The Purim Anthology.* Philadelphia: The Jewish Publication Society, 2003.

Internet Resources

http://www.earlyjewishwritings.com/esther.html
> This collection of Esther-related articles and commentary is suitable for anyone wishing to do further research.

http://www.holidays.net/purim/
> This Web site details the celebration of Purim, from its history to its celebration in modern times.

http://www.jewfaq.org/holiday9.htm
> This site explains how to celebrate Purim, giving dates for Purim along with a recipe for hamantachen. It also includes links to related sites.

http://www.jewishencyclopedia.com
> The complete contents of the 12-volume *Jewish Encyclopedia*, originally published 1901–1906, includes much information on Esther.

http://www.myjewishlearning.com
> This Web site provides well-written historical and scholarly information about Judaism, including articles about Esther.

http://www.ou.org/chagim/purim/default.htm

This site contains many articles of interest to adults concerning Purim. Written by rabbis, it includes much material for self-study.

http://www.sacred-texts.com

The Internet Sacred Text Archive has an enormous repository of electronic texts about religion, mythology, legends and folklore, and occult and esoteric topics. Texts related to Esther include the Vulgate and Mishna versions of the story; *The Legends of the Jews*, by Louis Ginzberg; the Talmudic writings (Babylonian) concerning the Scroll of Esther, along with the rabbinic discussion about the proper celebration of Purim; and the works of the ancient historians Herodotus (484–425 B.C.E.) and Flavius Josephus (37–100 C.E.).

http://www.yeshuatyisrael.com/Purim.htm

This site includes information about Purim, and includes a link to a beautifully illustrated story of Megillah Esther in PDF format.

Index

Abraham, 7, 8
Achaemenid dynasty, 33
   See also Persian Empire
Additions (Septuagint), 14–17, 20,
   43, 48, 55, 60, 103
Esther's prayers, 63–64
   Jews' rights, 93–94
   mention of God in the, 63
   Mordecai's dream, 27–28, 101
   Mordecai's genealogy, 29
   See also Esther (book)
Agag of the Amalekites (King), 46,
   48, 49
Ahashwerosh. See Ahasuerus (King)
Ahasuerus (King), 11, 18, 61, 101
   chooses Esther as queen, 13
   edict of, about wives, 39, 49
   edict of, for servants to bow to
      Haman, 48–49
   Esther's approach of, 64–65
   and Esther's banquets, 66–69,
      82–83
   and Haman's plan to kill the Jews,
      50–56, 83–86, 89–90
   harem of, 40–42
   and Jews' rights, 91–94, 96–97
   party of, 30–31, 34–38, 45–46
   plot of palace guards to kill,
      28–29, 42–44, **74**, 75
   and Queen Vashti's disobedience,
      12–13, 37–38

   rewards Mordecai, 75–80
   rewards of, after Haman's death,
      86, 88–89
   suspicions of, about Esther, 73–74
   wealth of, 88
Ahuramazda, 34
Alexander the Great, 18, 32, 33
Alpha text (AT), 17–18, 82–83
   See also Esther (book)
Amalekites, 46–48, 49
Anderson, Bernhard, 29
apocalyptic literature, 29
Apocrypha, 15
Artabanus, 61
Artaxerxes I, **35**

Bagathan, 28–29, 43, **74**, 75
Battle of Salamis, 32, 74
Bechtel, Carol M., 12, 25, 39, 42, 49,
   53, 63, 67, 81, 94, 101–102
Benjamin, 40, 48
Berg, Sandra Beth, 23, 53, 62
Berlin, Adele, 30, 32, 34, 38, 61, 72,
   77, 95
   and comic elements of Esther, 25,
      31, 75
   and date of Esther's writing, 18
   and God in the book of Esther, 59
   and the Persian Empire, 52–53,
      84–85
   and Purim, 22

Numbers in **bold italics** refer to captions.

116 Esther

and violence in the book of Esther, 97
Book of Maccabees, 99

Cambyses, 33
Cleopatra, 101
coincidence, 75–76
Council of Jamnia, 20
Cyrus the Great, *13*, 33, 86, 88

Darius I, *31*, 33–34, *95*
David, 78
"Day of Mordecai." *See* Purim
Dead Sea Scrolls, 20, *21*
Deuteronomy (Old Testament book), 8, *47*
Dositheus, 101

Elam, 24, 33
Eliezer, Pirke de-Rabbi, 77
Essene community, 19–20, *21*
Esther, *10*, *58*
　approaches Ahasuerus for help, 63–64
　banquets of, for Ahasuerus and Haman, 66–69, 82–83
　beauty of, 42, *43*
　chosen as queen by Ahasuerus, 13, 42, 44
　and fasting, 62–63
　and Haman's plot to kill the Jews, 59–63, 81, 83–86, 89–90
　in the harem, 40–42
　Jewish heritage of, 13
　and new edict for Jews' rights, 91–93, 96–97
　and Purim, 101
　requests mercy from Ahasuerus, 82–84, 89
　reveals Haman's plot, 85
　reward of, after Haman's death, 86, 88–89
　wealth of, 6, 86, 88–89, 103
　See also Esther (book)
Esther (book)
　Ahasuerus's edict about wives, 39
　Ahasuerus's party, 30–31, 35–36, 37, 38, 45–46
　Ahasuerus's plan to reward Mordecai, 77, 78
　as an etiology for Purim, 20–22, 98–99
　authorship of, 16–19
　and the Biblical Canon, 19–20
　as burlesque comedy, 25, 31, 39, 75, 95
　Esther reveals Haman's plot, 85
　Esther's banquet for Ahasuerus and Haman, 67, 68
　and Esther's beauty, *43*
　and Esther's coronation, *44*
　and Esther's fasting, 6
　and Esther's request for mercy, 82, 83–84, 89, 90
　genre of, 25–26
　God in the, 14, 19–20, 25, 29, 59, 60, 62, 81, 103
　guards' plan to kill Ahasuerus, 42–44, *74*, 75
　Haman's death, 86
　Haman's plan for revenge on Mordecai, 72
　and Haman's plan to kill the Jews, 51, 54, 55, 89
　and Haman's villainy, 34
　and Jews' rights, 91–92
　Mordecai asks Esther for help, 60, 61
　Mordecai's genealogy, 29
　and Persians' conversion to Judaism, 94
　placement of, in bibles, 11, 14–15
　Queen Vashti's disobedience, 25, 37, 38
　similarities of, to other literature, 23–25
　versions of, 12, 14–18, 19–20, 22, 102–103
　violence in, 20, 92–93, 97
　See also Additions (Septuagint); Esther; Masoretic text (MT)

faith
　and wealth, 7–9
Five Festal Scrolls, 11
Flavius Josephus. *See* Josephus

Fox, Michael V., 24, 30, 39, 41, 49, 90, 92, 98–99
  book of Esther genre, 25–26
  book of Esther versions, 17–18
  and God in the book of Esther, 62
  and hostility toward Jews in Persia, 54, 56
  and Jewish laws, 52

Gabriel (angel), 73
Ginzberg, Louis, 34–35, 36–37, 40, 49, 56, 64, 69, 71, 75, 80, 85
  See also legends, Jewish
God
  mention of, in Esther, 14, 19–20, 25, 29, 59, 60, 62, 81, 103
  mention of, in the Additions, 63
Greek Alpha text (AT), 17–18, 82–83
  See also Esther (book)

Haggadah, 28
  See also legends, Jewish
Haman, 28–29, 37, 43, 45–46
  death of, 86, **87**
  desire of, for reward, 77–79
  and Esther's banquets, 66–69, 82–83
  Mordecai's refusal to bow to, 48–50, 52, 63
  and plan to take revenge on Mordecai, 69–71, 76–77, 80–81
  plot of, to kill the Jews, 6, 14, 50–57, 59–63, 81, 83–86, 89–90
  sons of, 96–97
  wealth of, 88
Hammedatha the Agagite, 46
Harbonah, 86
harems, 40–42
Hathach, 60
Hegai, 41, 42
Herodotus, **36**, 70, 74

Ishtar, 24
Israel, 8–9, **13**, 29, 93
  and the Amalekites, 46–48, 49
  See also Jews

Jerome, 15
Jesus, 7, 9
Jews
  and the Babylonian captivity, **13**, 21, **24**
  in battle, 95–98
  and the Canon of Scripture, 19–20
  and the Diaspora, 23, 25, 26
  and edict for Jews' rights, 91–98
  Haman's plot to kill the, 6, 14, 50–57, 59–63, 81, 83–86, 89–90
  ill feeling toward, in Persia, 41, 42, 46
  and legends, 28
  and nationalistic fervor, 18
  See also Israel; legends, Jewish
Josephus, 17, 60, 73, 75, 77, 86, 88
Judah, **13**
Judith (book), 25

ketuvim, 11
  See also Tanakh (Hebrew bible)
Kurash. *See* Cyrus the Great
Kyshayarsha, 30

legends, Jewish, 28, 39, 40, 42, 56, 64, 75, 77, 85
  Ahasuerus's parties, 30, 34–35, 36–37
  Mordecai and Haman, 49, 69, 71, 79–80
Lots. *See* Purim
Lowell, James Russell, 76
Luther, Martin, **16**
Lysimachus, 101

Maccabean Period, 18
Marduk, 24
Masoretes, 12
Masoretic text (MT), 12–14, 15, 17, 30, 43, 55, 65, 66, 92
  and God's presence, 29, 60, 83, 103
  and Purim origins, 94
  See also Esther (book)
Megabyzys, 61
Memucan, 38–39

Mesopotamia, 24
Michael (archangel), 64, 73, 79
Midrash, 28, 30, 35, 37, 39, 42, 56, 77, 79–80
  See also legends, Jewish
Moore, Carey, 20, 25, 68, 92–93
Mordecai, 13, 40–41, 42, 103
  as book of Esther author, 19
  genealogy of, 29, 48
  as grand vizier, 89
  and Haman's plot to kill the Jews, 6, 14, 57, 59–62, 86
  Haman's revenge on, 69–71
  as hero in the book of Esther, 93
  and Jews' rights, 91–96
  and mourning, 57, 59–60, 80
  and Purim, 98, 101
  refusal of, to bow to Haman, 48–50, 52, 63
  reward of, after Haman's death, 86, 89
  thwarts plan of guards to kill Ahasuerus, 27–29, 43–44, 46, *74*, 75
  wealth of, 6, 86, 89
Moses, *47*
mourning, 57, 59–60, 63, 80

Nebuchadnezzar, *13*
New Testament, 7, 9, 12

Old Testament, 7–9, 12, *16*, 23, 25, 46, *47*, 48, 54, 76, 78, 94
book of Esther in the, 11, 14
  See also Esther (book)

Persepolis, *13*, *31*, 33, 34, **70**
Persian Empire, *13*, 18, 19, 21, 25, 29, 32–34, 52, 84–85, 88–89, 93–95
Phylacus, 74
Protestant Reformation, 15
Proto-Esther, 17
  See also Esther (book)
Ptolemy, 101
pur (lot), 50
  See also Purim
Purim, 11–12, 14, 20–22, 26, 31, *47*, 91, 93, 94
  establishment of, 98–102

Qumran, 19–20, *21*

Rembrandt, *83*

Samuel, 46
Saul, 46, 48
Scroll of Esther, 11–12, 29, **100**
  See also Esther (book)
Septuagint, 14–17, 99
  See also Additions (Septuagint)
Shaashgaz, 42
Solomon, 8–9, 78
Susa (Persian city), 9, 30, 32–34, 37, 56, 62, 78, 94, 96, 97–98

Talmud, 28, 102
Tanakh (Hebrew bible), 11, 12, 28
Targum Sheni, 17
  See also Esther (book)
Thares, 28–29, 43, **74**, 75
Theomestor, 74
Torah, *16*, 21, 28

Vashti (Queen), 12–13, 25, 30, 37–39, **44**, 49
Vulgate, 15

wealth
  of Esther, 6, 86, 88–89, 103
  and faith, 7–9
  in the Persian Empire, 34
"The Writings" (ketuvim), 11
  See also Tanakh (Hebrew bible)

Xerxes (Ahasuerus). See Ahasuerus (King)
Xerxes Gate, **70**
Xerxes I (ruler of Persia), 18, 30, *31*, 32–34, 61

Zeresh (wife of Haman), 70, 71, 72, 80
Zoroastrianism, 34

Illustration Credits

2: Erich Lessing/Art Resource, NY
10: Esther, c.1869 (oil on canvas) by Jean Francois Portaels (1818-95), Art Gallery of New South Wales, Sydney, Australia / The Bridgeman Art Library
12: Used under license from Shutterstock, Inc.
13: Used under license from Shutterstock, Inc.
15: Used under license from Shutterstock, Inc.
16: © 2009 Jupiterimages Corporation
16: Used under license from Shutterstock, Inc.
21: Used under license from Shutterstock, Inc.
22: Used under license from Shutterstock, Inc.
24: Used under license from Shutterstock, Inc.
31: Used under license from Shutterstock, Inc.
34: Used under license from Shutterstock, Inc.
35: Erich Lessing/Art Resource, NY
36: © 2009 Jupiterimages Corporation
43: Queen Esther, 1878 (oil on canvas) by Edwin Longsden Long (1829-91), National Gallery of Victoria, Melbourne, Australia/The Bridgeman Art Library
44: The Art Archive/Galleria d'Arte Moderna Rome/Alfredo Dagli Orti
47: Bildarchiv Preussischer Kulturbesitz/Art Resource, NY
51: Ahasuerus and Haman (oil on canvas) by Aert de Gelder (1645-1727), The Barber Institute of Fine Arts, University of Birmingham/ The Bridgeman Art Library
58: Reunion des Musees Nationaux/Art Resource, NY
65: Reunion des Musees Nationaux/Art Resource, NY
68: Used under license from Shutterstock, Inc.
69: Scala/Art Resource, NY
70: Used under license from Shutterstock, Inc.
74: Used under license from Shutterstock, Inc.
79: Used under license from Shutterstock, Inc.
83: © 2009 Jupiterimages Corporation
87: Ms 1 fol.284r Esther and Ahasuerus and the Hanging of Haman, from the Souvigny Bible (vellum) by French School (12th century). Bibliotheque Municipale, Moulins, France/Lauros/Giraudon/The Bridgeman Art Library
95: Used under license from Shutterstock, Inc.
96: Bildarchiv Preussischer Kulturbesitz/Art Resource, NY
99: Used under license from Shutterstock, Inc.
100: Used under license from Shutterstock, Inc.
102: Used under license from Shutterstock, Inc.

Cover photo: Esther (oil on canvas) by Hermann Anschuetz (1802-80), Pushkin Museum, Moscow, Russia/The Bridgeman Art Library

STEPHEN B. WOODRUFF is a 29-year veteran of the elementary school classroom, having taught grades 4 to 6. Mr. Woodruff is also a freelance writer of children's literature and has published several magazine stories and articles. He holds a master's degree in education from SUNY Plattsburgh and attended Princeton Theological Seminary (1977–1978). Mr. Woodruff lives in Morrisonville, New York, with his wife, Jeanette, and his three children, Erik, Rachael, and Andrew.